A GUIDED TOUR OF FIVE WORKS BY PLATO

Also by Christopher Biffle:

The Castle of Pearl: A Guide to Self-Knowledge

Turning Your Life Around (with David Toma)

A Journey through Your Childhood

Garden in the Snowy Mountains

*A Guided Tour of René Descartes'
Meditations on First Philosophy*
with a complete translation of
the *Meditations* by Ronald Rubin.

*A Guided Tour of Selections from
Aristotle's Nicomachean Ethics*

Software:

*Time Throttle: A Multicultural Tour
of the World, 600 B.C.–1400 A.D.*

Also in the Guided Tour Series:

*A Guided Tour of John Stuart Mill's
Utilitarianism* (Julius Jackson, author)

A GUIDED TOUR OF FIVE WORKS BY PLATO

Second Edition

with complete translations of
Euthyphro, Apology,
Crito, Phaedo (Death Scene),
and "Allegory of the Cave"

Christopher Biffle
Crafton Hills College

Mayfield Publishing Company
Mountain View, California
London • Toronto

About the Translation: The text is based upon Benjamin Jowett's classic 19th-century translation. Christopher Biffle has revised the punctuation and substituted words and phrases more appropriate for the modern reader.

Library of Congress Cataloging-in-Publication Data

Biffle, Christopher
   A guided tour of five works by Plato: with complete translations of Euthyphro, Apology, Crito, Phaedo (death scene), and "Allegory of the Cave" / Christopher Biffle.
      p.   cm.
   Includes bibliographical references.
   ISBN 1-55934-356-7
   1. Socrates. 2. Idea (Philosophy) 3. Good and evil. I. Plato.
II. Title.
B317.B53 1994
184—dc20   94-29164
                                                      CIP

Manufactured in the United States of America
10 9 8 7 6 5 4 3 2 1

Mayfield Publishing Company
1280 Villa Street
Mountain View, California 94041

Sponsoring editor, James Bull; production editor, Larisa North; manuscript editor, Joan Pendleton; cover designer, Jean Mailander. The text was set in 10/12 Palatino by Execustaff Composition Services and printed on 50# Thor Smooth by Malloy Lithographing, Inc.

This book is printed on acid-free, recycled paper.

CONTENTS

PREFACE

To the Teacher

I wanted students to bring their books to class as full of underlinings and margin notes as mine. Before I stitched everything together in lecture, I wanted my students to read and re-read challenging passages and try to unravel them on their own. I wanted them to come to class with a lot to say. I finally realized that I needed an edition of Plato's dialogues designed for the novice in philosophy. The text would contain the dialogues surrounded by tasks that would move students to philosophical thinking, reading and writing.

My philosophy students need a lot of practice in orderly thinking and writing. They need practice in following a logical pattern, giving reasons for assertions, clarifying points with examples, and quoting supporting material from a text. There is plenty of practice here. I collect xeroxed copies of these pages from the students infrequently, but unannounced, and grade them quickly, as a tennis coach would grade practice swings. I also find it useful to complete parts of the tour in class discussion. Most effective is to assign a writing task on a given section to pairs of students for cooperative work in class. It is a fine occupation to listen to the pleasant racket of novices arguing philosophy.

The truth is most students will read Plato's dialogues only once in their lives. We need to slow down that precious reading and make it as fruitful as possible. The reading and writing tasks

I have incorporated in this book are designed to help students underline, write in the margins, re-read, paraphrase, outline, and eventually analyze philosophical classics in an orderly way. This method will require more of the students' time to get through the dialogues, but because students do so much more of the work, it will take instructors about the same time to teach.

The reading assignments (Annotation Tasks) in this book are more elementary than the writing assignments. What is completed on first reading should be elementary: identifying characters and finding the main outline of the argument. By the end of the book, the student will receive fewer hints about what to do while reading and larger problems to solve in writing. To paraphrase Teilhard de Chardin, the goal of the book is also the goal of life: to see.

New to the Second Edition

In this edition, the Jowett translation has been updated and more annotation tasks have been added. "A Visual Introduction to Philosophy" is also new. It introduces key vocabulary terms and provides a schematic view of some of the major branches of philosophy. It can be assigned at any point during your use of this book. Finally, I've added more than 100 critical thinking tasks disguised as quiz items.

I'd like to thank the following reviewers for helping me correct the weaknesses in the first edition: Don Porter, College of San Mateo; Merrill Ring, California State University, Fullerton; Theresa H. Sandok, Bellarmine College; and Emily Teipe, Fullerton College. Any problems that remain are due to my inability to follow their good advice.

I wish everyone could share in my delight at a completely new edition. My dear Alea Biffle Southard . . . Grandpa can't wait to learn what you'll teach him.

To the Student

I want you to understand Plato and not be bored. This book is a tour of Plato's dialogues. I point things out, and then we consider them together.

I want this book to accomplish for you what the best teacher I ever had, Harry Berger at the University of California at Santa Cruz, accomplished for me. He asked good questions in the right order and showed me the pleasure of thinking clearly. The tasks in this book will help you read, think, and write more clearly about philosophy. Read slowly in a quiet place. All you will need for your journey is a pen.

Christopher Biffle

This book is dedicated to Harry Berger, Jr.

E poiche la sua mano alla mia pose,
con lieto volto, ond io mi confortai.
Mi mise dentro alle segrete cose.

Dante

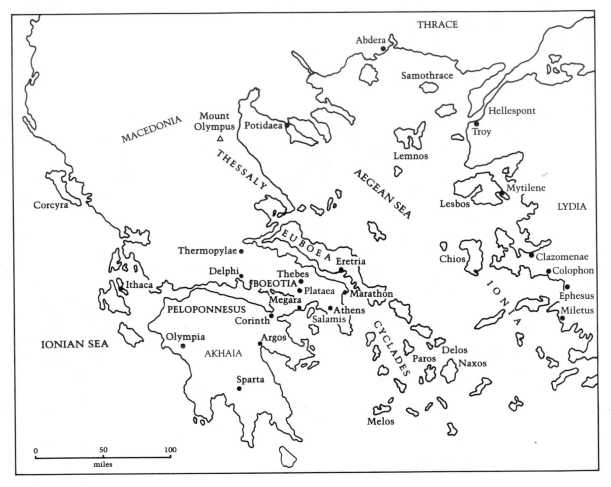

The Greek Mainland

INTRODUCTION

Preparing for the Tour

The best tours have no timetables. The traveler stops at will to ponder the broad and strange horizon. On this tour you are encouraged to dally. Underline, make notes in the margin, fill in the blanks, push your chair back from the table, and reflect upon the new world spread before you.

Thinking about things is a pleasure. Aristotle believed there was no higher pleasure. The design of this book encourages you to be thoughtfully active. On the journey ahead you may discover not only Plato, but also the pleasure of your own reflections.

Here is our itinerary:

- We begin with a brief introduction to Socrates, Plato, and the history of Athens.

- Then we start our guided tour with Plato's *Euthyphro,* in which we witness Socrates in action as he tries to help an acquaintance, Euthyphro, think more clearly.

- Next on the tour is Plato's *Apology,* in which we listen to Socrates' defense while he is on trial for his life.

- In the *Crito,* we observe Socrates in jail, sentenced to death. His old friend Crito tries to convince him to escape.

- In the next section, from the end of Plato's *Phaedo,* we watch Socrates meet his death.

- Finally, in the "Allegory of the Cave" from Plato's *Republic,* we encounter a brief but rich summary of Plato's vision of the universe, the philosopher, and society.

Socrates and Athens

According to Plato, his student and biographer, Socrates had a pug nose, ample belly, and bulging eyes. His beauty, according to Plato, was hidden within. Socrates did not agree; he always held that, if the hidden beauty was wisdom, he had none. However, he might say you could not understand him without understanding his city, Athens.

Athens was a *polis*, a state that was a small city. Other Greek cities, such as Sparta, Thebes, and Corinth, were city-states as well. Each was a law and a political system unto itself. Imagine that New York was ruled by a king, Philadelphia by a democratic government, and Boston by a curious mixture of the two, and you have an idea of the nature of the Greek city-states.

Athens, of course, was the democracy. Democracy grew slowly in the several hundred years before Socrates' birth. The movement began when Draco published the laws of the state in 621 B.C. This is significant because written laws are less subject to the whim of judge or ruler than is a malleable body of traditional practices. Solon and Cleistenes in the sixth century B.C. gave larger groups of citizens direct access to Athenian political processes. By the middle of the fifth century B.C., the Golden Age of Pericles, a democratic system, more radical than our own in some ways, was fully established. Although women, slaves, and foreigners had no vote, the 40,000 free men had amazing power. In the United States our representatives make decisions for us. If we ourselves could vote to go to war, to make peace, to ratify a treaty, to raise or lower taxes, or to enact any other major policy decision, then we would be as democratic as was Socrates' Athens.

Besides the growth of democracy, the other major event in the early life of Athens was the victory over the Persian empire. In two wars Athens, united with other Greek city-states, defeated the Persian Goliath through cunning, bravery, and what the Athenians held to be a superior political system. The Greeks were free and fought by choice. According to the Greek historian, Herodotus, the Persians had to drive their soldiers into battle with whips.

It is simple to state the chronology of events that led to the rise of democracy and the fall of the Persians. It is more difficult to convey to you the incredible constellation of brilliant individuals who lived in Athens in the fifth and fourth centuries B.C. Imagine a single, fabulous city, fill it with some of the greatest geniuses of all time, and then compare this impossible dream city with Socrates' Athens.

Walking through the marketplace of the finest city we can imagine, we might find Isaac Newton discussing the nature of God with Tolstoy. Along the narrow streets we can look into the studios of Picasso, Leonardo da Vinci, and Vincent van Gogh. A young Charles Dickens sits in a coffee shop with Galileo. The Wright brothers, with bicycle parts in a wheelbarrow, wave their greeting from the crowded street. In a grove of green, glistening alders Julius Caesar addresses a crowd, and in that noisy crowd Michelangelo and Richard the Lionhearted exchange views on the speaker's merits. Isadora Duncan leads a group of her students, like a cloud of bright butterflies, among the latest black-bronze statues of the city's most famous sculptor, Auguste Rodin. Her group argues among themselves about the virtues of his latest work, "The Thinker." In a theater outside the city you can see world-premiere presentations of works by an interesting new talent, William Shakespeare. On a hill at the center of the won-drous city, Frank Lloyd Wright guides the completion of a cluster of white marble temples. Within a small courtyard crowded with stunned onlookers, a bespectacled German mathematician, Albert Einstein, discusses the curvature of space. And the popular leader of this menagerie of genius? Let us imagine it is Teddy Roosevelt.

Now, if you were born in such a city, believed its laws were the most just on earth, owed your entire education and upbring-ing to it, and had fought to defend it in a long war, you might prefer to die, as Socrates did, rather than leave.

Socrates' Athens was probably even more astonishing than our imaginary city. We had to ransack the ages and three continents to fill our dream. Athens, 2,500 years ago, never had a popula-tion larger than 250,000.

During the fifth and fourth centuries B.C., fifteen of the world's most influential geniuses could be found in Athens. Aeschylus, Sophocles, Aristophanes, and Euripides are still among the world's most influential playwrights. Countless buildings have been mod-eled after the Parthenon and its sister temples on the Acropolis, which were designed by the Athenians Ictinus and Callicrates. Although Phidias' Athena, a 40-foot miracle of gold and ivory has not survived, there are 10,000 copies of the statues of Praxiteles. Pericles ranks among the greatest of the world's leaders; historians are indebted to Thucydides and Herodotus, as are doctors to Hippocrates; and, of course, there are Socrates, Plato, and Aristotle.

If every hint of the influence of these fifteen Greek men and their achievements were removed from our world, we would be barbarians.

Socrates lived through the glory of Athens and in his last days was at the center of her tragedy. He was born about 470 B.C. and never recorded his own philosophy. Virtually all we know about him comes from three sources: Plato, Xenophon, and the playwright Aristophanes. Moreover, these three sources offer different accounts. For example, Aristophanes' Socrates in *The Clouds* is a fool. Plato's account, however, is by far the most historically influential.

According to Plato, Socrates served with distinction in the Peloponnesian war between Athens and Sparta. He married Xanthippe, fathered three children, preferred living in poverty, and spent most of his days talking in the marketplace. His favorite subjects, virtue and values, had not previously been investigated systematically.

Philosophy itself was hardly two centuries old in Socrates' day. In about 600 B.C. the first philosopher, Thales, declared that the basic substance of the universe was water. This began philosophy, because previous definitions of the universe relied on religion, myth, and story for explanation. Philosophers before Socrates were concerned mainly with trying to define the one thing that united the many different aspects of the universe. Socrates drove philosophy inward and urged his fellow Athenians to think about their souls.

This new turn in philosophy may have been in response to the sophists, a group of teachers who offered to show anyone with money how to be influential in the Assembly. Their concern was not with truth or spiritual values but with reputation. Protagoras, one of the chief sophists, held that every individual's opinion is equally correct. Therefore, if Truth is unreachable, the individual can do no better than seek Acclaim.

In the first dialogues Plato wrote, including *Euthyphro, Apology,* and *Crito,* Socrates held that if the majority hold a belief, that belief is likely to be wrong. Or, to put it another way, Acclaim is philosophical death.

Plato maintained this position in the "Allegory of the Cave." The real philosopher is the outsider, the outlaw. The more a person is honored and considered wise by society, the less that person is in contact with Truth. The true philosopher persistently delivers an unpopular message, often at his own peril.

Socrates was sentenced to die by an Athenean court in 399 B.C. The court consisted of a large group of free male citizens. One of the most popular interpretations of Socrates' death holds that he had the wrong friends. One friend, Alcibiades, was first a flamboyant hero and then a notorious traitor during Athens' long war with Sparta (which ended with Athens defeated). Charmides and Critias (relatives of Plato) and Theramenes were among the "Thirty" who established a tyrannical but short-lived government in Athens after her defeat. According to this interpretation, the charges against Socrates of impiety and of corrupting the young were a smokescreen for his real crime—previous association with enemies of the state. The problem with this view is that it makes Plato's portrait of Socrates irrelevant.

Socrates may indeed have had the wrong friends, but this is not mentioned in the four works ahead on our tour. In fact,

Socrates is terribly alone in these four dialogues. We may never know the real Socrates; he may well have been less fascinating than Plato's portrait of him. Your task will be to construct your interpretation of Plato's interpretation.

Before we learn more about Plato, write down what you remember about Socrates and his Athens. (Complete the following statements in the spaces provided.)

Important events in the early history of Athens were _____

_____

_____ . What was unique about Athens during its Golden Age was the "constellation of brilliant individuals." The ones I remember are _____

_____

_____

_____

_____ . The major events in Socrates' life were _____

_____

_____

_____

_____ . In reading Plato's account of Socrates, I hope to find out _____

_____

_____

_____

_____ .

Plato and the Dialogues

According to many scholars, most of what we know about Plato comes from his own *Seventh Epistle*. Unlike Socrates, he was born into a noble Athenian family, who reportedly traced its ancestry to the god Poseidon. His intense interest in politics began early in life, but the experiences of his relatives, Charmides and Critias, as members of the tyrannical Thirty and, more importantly, Socrates' death dissuaded him from entering the political arena.

After Socrates' death, Plato recorded the activities of his teacher in dialogues like the *Euthyphro*. In these early dialogues Socrates attempts to be instructive by being destructive. For example, a central term (in the *Euthyphro* it is *holiness*) is defined in a variety of ways by Socrates' partners, and Socrates, in turn, shows how these definitions are unsatisfactory. In the *Apology* and the *Crito*, Plato records events from Socrates' last days. The former relates Socrates' defense at his trial, and the latter occurs one morning in his prison cell. To say much more about these would spoil the journey ahead.

After a trip to Italy and Sicily (where Plato may have encountered a group of Pythagorean philosophers), Plato established his now famous Academy in Athens. Complete with distinguished visiting scholars and students, the Academy is now considered the first university. During this period, Plato wrote works like the *Republic*, in which Socrates is the main speaker. Many scholars believe that the substance of these doctrines is more clearly Plato's own. The "Allegory of the Cave" is one of the most famous sections of the *Republic* and presents perhaps the most brilliant philosophical synopsis ever written.

In 367 and 361 B.C. Plato returned to Sicily to attempt to put some of his political ideas into practice. He was urged to make the journeys by Dion, brother-in-law of Dionysius the Younger, the ruler of Syracuse. Both trips were a failure due to political intrigue, and the last one nearly cost Plato his life. These incidents and his establishment of the Academy are important because they show us Plato was not an idle theorizer about education and politics.

In the last years of Plato's life, his dialogues took a new turn. Socrates is no longer an important figure as Plato addresses problems raised by his previous works. Plato remained at the Academy until his death in 347 B.C.

At this point in the tour, do not confuse the importance of Plato with that of the philosophers before him, including Socrates. We have very little of the works of Thales and other philosophers before Socrates. What we do have indicates they were concerned mainly with one question: What is the one thing underlying the many apparently different aspects of reality? Socrates wrote nothing, and without Plato may not have been long remembered. It is Plato's portrait of him, largely in the dialogues you are about to travel through, that made him philosophy's saint. Plato was not the first philosopher but the first complete philosopher. He raised questions about the universe, ethics, aesthetics, political philosophy, education, and science. The philosophers before him, including Socrates, faintly sketched the Temple of Philosophy; Plato constructed the ground floor.

Looking Back

On this tour we keep looking back to see more clearly where we are. The first section of our tour is almost complete. What notes do you need to make to help you remember our journey thus far?

The main things I want to remember about Socrates and the history of Athens are _____

_____

_____

_____

_____ . What I need to remember about Plato is _____

_____

_____

_____

_____ .

What do you think of the tour so far?

_____

_____

_____

_____

_____ .

At the next stop on our tour, we witness a tragic drama in four acts, in which the hero is, of course, Socrates of Athens.

/1/ *EUTHYPHRO*

Preview

In the last weeks of his life, Socrates meets an acquaintance, Euthyphro, outside the court. The main theme of their dialogue is the definition of holiness.

Thus far on our tour you have responded thoughtfully to my questions. In each of the following five works by Plato, you will be underlining and making notes in the book's margins. These Annotation Tasks will help you understand the general concepts of each dialogue. Then, after each selection, we will have a dialogue of our own to help you more clearly comprehend Socrates and the philosophy of Plato.

In the *Euthyphro* the Annotation Tasks involve finding background information and understanding the main theme of the dialogue.

Annotation Tasks

Background Information.   Every piece of literature introduces characters and provides information about their world. Important pieces of this information usually appear in the first few pages. In the *Euthyphro* you will have no trouble finding Euthyphro's and Socrates' reasons for coming to court. You will have to read slowly, however, to find information about the differences in their personalities. Search for examples of Socrates' use of irony. Start by underlining anything he says that sounds mocking or not entirely serious. Underline Euthyphro's profession and anything he says that gives you clues about his character.

Main Theme. Once you are past the opening pages of the dialogue, the Annotation Tasks will help you find each definition of holiness and the main points Socrates makes to improve and/or refute each definition.

Euthyphro

EUTHYPHRO: Why have you left the Lyceum, Socrates, and what are you doing by the court of the king archon? Surely you cannot be engaged in an action before the king, as I am.[1]

SOCRATES: Not in an action, Euthyphro. Indictment is the word the Athenians use.

EUTH: What! I suppose someone is prosecuting you; I cannot believe you are prosecuting someone else.

SOC: Certainly not.

EUTH: Then someone else is prosecuting you?

SOC: Yes.

EUTH: Who is he?

SOC: A young man who is little known, Euthyphro, and whom I hardly know. His name is Meletus of the township of Pitthis. Perhaps you know his appearance. He has a beaklike nose, long straight hair, and straggly beard.

EUTH: No, I do not remember him, Socrates. What is the charge he brings against you?

SOC: What is the charge? Well, a very serious charge, which shows a good deal of character in the young man, and for which he is certainly to be respected. He says he knows how the youth are corrupted and who are their corruptors. I believe he must be a wise man, and seeing I am anything but a wise man, he has discovered me and is going to accuse me of corrupting his young friends. Of this our mother the State is to be the judge. Of all our political men he is the only one who seems to me to begin in the right way, with the cultivation of virtue in the youth. He is a good farmer who takes care of the young shoots first and clears away us who are their destroyers. That is the first step; he will afterwards attend to the elder branches, and if he goes on as he has begun, he will be a very great public benefactor.

EUTH: I hope he may, but I fear, Socrates, the reverse will turn out to be the truth. My opinion is in attacking you he is simply aiming a blow at the very heart of the city. But in what way does he say you corrupt the young?

SOC: He brings a strange charge against me, which at first hearing is surprising. He says I am an inventor of new gods and deny the existence of old ones. This is the basis of his indictment.

EUTH: I understand, Socrates. He intends to attack you about the spiritual sign which occasionally, as you say, comes to you.

Underline:
1. Socrates' reason for being at court.
2. Meletus' charge against Socrates.
3. Examples of Socrates' irony.

Socrates' ironic opinion of Meletus is _____ _____ _____ _____ _____.

9

Underline:
1. Two indications of Euthyphro's profession.
2. Euthyphro's purpose in court.
3. Examples of Socratic irony.

He thinks you have unorthodox beliefs and is going to bring you before the court for this. He knows such a charge is readily received, for the world is always jealous of novelties in religion. I know when I speak in the Assembly about divine things, and foretell the future to them, they laugh at me as if I was a madman. Yet every word I say is true. But they are jealous of all of us; I suppose we must be brave and not mind them.

SOC: Their laughter, friend Euthyphro, is not important. A man may be thought wise, but the Athenians, I suspect, do not care much about this, until he begins to make other men wise. Then for some reason, perhaps, as you say from jealousy, they are angry.

EUTH: I have no wish to discover their attitude toward me about this.

SOC: Perhaps you don't mingle with the masses and are not likely to impart your wisdom. But I have a benevolent habit of pouring myself out to everybody and would even pay for a listener, and I am afraid that the Athenians know this. Therefore, as I was saying, if the Athenians would only laugh at me as you say they laugh at you, the time might pass pleasantly enough in the court. But perhaps they are serious, and then what the end will be only you prophets can predict.

EUTH: I believe the affair will end in nothing, Socrates, and you will win your case. And I think I shall win mine.

SOC: And what is your case? Are you the prosecutor or defendant, Euthyphro?

EUTH: I am the prosecutor.

SOC: Of whom?

EUTH: You will think me mad when I tell you whom I am prosecuting.

SOC: Why, will the criminal fly off?

EUTH: No, he is not very lively at his time of life.

SOC: Who is he?

EUTH: My father.

SOC: Your father! Good heavens, you don't mean that?

EUTH: Yes.

SOC: Of what is he accused?

EUTH: Murder, Socrates.

SOC: By the powers, Euthyphro! How little does the common herd know about what is right in such a case. A man must be an extraordinary man and have made great strides in wisdom before he could have been able to bring this charge.

EUTH: Indeed, Socrates, he must have made great strides.

SOC: I suppose the man whom your father murdered was one of your relatives. If he had been a stranger you would never think of prosecuting him.

Socrates' general attitude toward

Euthyphro is _____

_____

_____

_____ .

EUTH: I am amused, Socrates, at your distinction between one who is a relation and one who is not a relation. For surely the pollution is the same in either case if you knowingly associate with the murderer when you ought to cleanse yourself and him by bringing him to court.

The real question is whether the murdered man has been justly slain. If justly, then your duty is to let the matter alone; but if unjustly, then even if the murderer lives under the same roof with you and eats at the same table, prosecute him. The man who is dead was a servant of mine who worked for us as a field laborer at Naxos. One day in a fit of drunken passion he got into a quarrel with one of our domestic servants and killed him. My father tied him hand and foot and threw him into a ditch, and then sent to Athens to ask of a priest what he should do with him. Meantime, my father had no thought of him, being under the impression the man was a murderer and that even if he did die there would be no great harm. This was just what happened. For such was the effect of cold, hunger and chains upon the laborer, he was dead before the messenger returned from the seer. My father and family are angry with me for taking the side of the murderer and prosecuting my father. They say he did not kill him, and if he did, the dead man was nothing but a murderer, and I should not take any notice, for a son is unholy who prosecutes a father. That shows, Socrates, how little they know of the opinions of the gods about the holy and the unholy.

In essence, Euthyphro is arguing that _____ _____ _____ _____ _____ _____ _____ .

SOC: Good heavens, Euthyphro! Have you such precise knowledge of the holy and the unholy, and of divine things in general, that you are not afraid you too may be doing an unholy thing bringing a case against your father?

EUTH: The best of Euthyphro, and that which distinguishes him, Socrates, from other men, is his exact knowledge of all these matters. What should I be good for without that?

SOC: Rare friend! I think I cannot do better than be your disciple, before the trial with Meletus begins. Then I shall challenge him, and say I have always had a great interest in religious questions, and now, as he charges me with innovations in religion, I am your disciple.

"Now you, Meletus," as I shall say to him, "acknowledge Euthyphro to be a great theologian and sound in his opinions. If you think that of him, you should think the same of me and not have me into court. You should begin by indicting my teacher who is the real corruptor, not of the young, but of the old; that is to say, of myself whom he instructs, and of his old father whom he admonishes and chastises." And if Meletus refuses to listen to me, but will go on, and will not shift the indictment from me to you, I cannot do better than say in court that I challenged him in this way.

Socrates wants Euthyphro to think _____ _____, but, in fact, Socrates means _____ _____ _____ . Therefore, this is another example of Socrates' irony.

Underline:
1. Euthyphro's first attempt at defining the holy.
2. Socrates' reaction to this attempt.

Euthyphro argues his action is

holy because _____

_____

_____

_____ .

Thus far, the main differences between Socrates and Euthyphro

are: _____

_____

_____

_____

_____

_____

_____ .

EUTH: Yes, Socrates, and if he attempts to indict me I will find his weak point. The court shall have a great deal more to say to him than to me.

SOC: I know that, dear friend, and that is the reason I desire to be your disciple. I observe no one, not even Meletus, appears to notice you. His sharp eyes have found me out immediately and he has indicted me for impiety. And therefore I beg you to tell me the nature of the holy and the unholy, which you said you knew so well. Is not holiness in every action always the same? And is not unholiness always the opposite of holiness and always the same in every case?

EUTH: Of course, Socrates.

SOC: Then what is holiness and what is unholiness?

EUTH: Holiness is doing as I am doing; prosecuting anyone who is guilty of murder, sacrilege, or of any other similar crime—whether he be your father or mother, or some other person, that makes no difference—and not prosecuting them is unholy. Please consider, Socrates, what a clear proof I will give you of the truth of what I am saying, which I have already given to others. For do not men regard Zeus as the best and most righteous of the gods?—and even they admit he bound his father (Cronos) because he wickedly devoured his sons, and he too had punished his own father (Uranus) for a similar reason, in a nameless manner.[2] And yet when I bring a case against my father, they are angry with me. This is their inconsistent way of talking when the gods are concerned and when I am concerned.

SOC: Is this the reason, Euthyphro, why I am charged with impiety—that I cannot get away with these stories about the gods? And therefore I suppose people think me wrong. But, as you who are well informed about the gods believe in them, I cannot do better than assent to your superior wisdom. For what else can I say, confessing as I do, that I know nothing of them. I wish you would tell me whether you really believe such stories are true.

EUTH: Yes, Socrates, and things more wonderful still, of which the world is in ignorance.

SOC: Do you really believe the gods fought with one another, had quarrels, battles, and the like, as the poets say, and as you may see represented in the works of great artists? The temples are full of them, especially the robe of Athena, embroidered with them, which is carried up to the Acropolis at the great Panathenaea.[3] Are all these tales of the gods true, Euthyphro?

EUTH: Yes, Socrates, and, as I was saying, I can tell you, if you would like to hear them, many other things about the gods which would amaze you.

SOC: I believe you. You shall tell me them at some other time when I have leisure. Right now I would rather hear from you a more precise answer, which you have not as yet given, my friend, to the question, "What is the holy?" In reply, you only say that holiness is doing as you do, charging your father with murder.

EUTH: And that is true, Socrates.

SOC: I am sure, Euthyphro, but there are many other holy acts.

EUTH: There are.

SOC: Remember I did not ask you to give me two or three examples of holiness, but to explain the essential characteristic or form which makes all holy actions to be holy. Do you not recollect that there was one essential characteristic or form which made the unholy unholy, and the holy holy?

EUTH: I remember.

SOC: Tell me what this is and then I shall have a standard which I may look at and by which I may measure the nature of actions, whether yours or anyone's, and say this action is holy, and that unholy.

EUTH: I will tell you, if you like.

SOC: I would like it very much.

EUTH: Holiness, then, is what the gods love, and unholiness is what the gods hate.

SOC: Very good, Euthyphro. You have now given me just the sort of answer I wanted. Whether it is true or not I cannot tell, although I believe you will show me the truth of your words.

EUTH: Of course.

SOC: Come, then, let us examine what we are saying. That thing or person which the gods love is holy and the thing or person which the gods hate is unholy. Was that what you said?

EUTH: Yes, I said that.

SOC: And that seems to have been very well said too?

EUTH: Yes, Socrates, I think so.

SOC: And further, Euthyphro, the gods were admitted to have enmities and hatreds and differences—that was also said?

EUTH: Yes, that was said.

SOC: And what sort of difference creates hatred and anger? Suppose for example you and I, my good friend, disagree about a number. Do differences of this sort make us enemies and set us against one another, or do we at once calculate and end them by a sum?

EUTH: We do.

SOC: Or, suppose we differ about the size of something, do we not quickly put that difference to an end by measuring?

EUTH: That is true.

SOC: And we end a controversy about heavy and light by using a scale?

EUTH: Of course.

SOC: But what are the disagreements which, because they cannot be thus decided, make us angry and set us against one

Underline:
1. The main points Socrates makes against the first definition of the holy.
2. Euthyphro's second definition of the holy.

Socrates' point about disagreements about numbers, size, and weight is _____ _____ _____ _____ .

another? I believe the answer does not occur to you at the moment and therefore I will suggest this happens when the disagreements are about the just and unjust, good and evil, honorable and dishonorable. Are not these the issues about which, when disagreeing, and unable satisfactorily to decide our disagreements, we quarrel?

EUTH: Yes, Socrates, that is the nature of the disagreements about which we quarrel.

SOC: And the quarrels of the gods, noble Euthyphro, when they occur, are they similar?

EUTH: They are.

SOC: They have differences of opinion, as you say, about good and evil, just and unjust, honorable and dishonorable. There would have been no quarrels among them, if there had been no such differences—would there?

EUTH: You are quite right.

SOC: Does not every man love what he believes noble and just and good and hate the opposite?

EUTH: Very true.

SOC: But then, as you say, people regard the same things differently, some as just and others as unjust; they argue about this and there arise wars and fights among them.

EUTH: Yes, that is true.

SOC: The same things are hated by some gods and loved by other gods and are both hateful and dear to them?

EUTH: True.

SOC: Then the same things, Euthyphro, will be holy and also unholy?

EUTH: That, I suppose, is true.

SOC: Then, my friend, I am surprised you have not answered what I asked. For I certainly did not ask what was both holy and unholy: And what is loved by the gods appears also to be hated by them. Therefore, Euthyphro, in bringing your father to trial you may very likely be doing what is agreeable to Zeus but disagreeable to Cronos or Uranus and what is acceptable to Hephaestus but unacceptable to Hera,[4] and there may be other gods who have similar differences of opinion.

EUTH: But I believe, Socrates, that all the gods would be agreed about the correctness of punishing a murderer. There would be no difference of opinion about that.

SOC: Well, but speaking of men, Euthyphro, did you ever hear anyone arguing that a murderer or any sort of evil-doer should be let off?

EUTH: They are always arguing this, especially in courts of law. They commit all sorts of crimes and there is nothing they will not do or say to escape punishment.

The differences between these disagreements and the previous is

_____

_____

_____

_____

_____ .

Underline this. It is an important point in Socrates' argument

against Euthyphro because _____

_____

_____

_____ .

Euthyphro's second definition of the holy is not satisfactory because

_____

_____

_____

_____

_____ .

SOC: But do they admit their guilt, Euthyphro, and yet say they ought not to be punished?

EUTH: No, they do not.

SOC: Then there are some things which they do not try to say and do. They do not try to argue the guilty are to be unpunished, but they deny their guilt, do they not?

EUTH: Yes.

SOC: Then they do not argue that the evil-doer should not be punished, but they argue about the fact of who the evil-doer is and what he did and when?

EUTH: True.

SOC: And the gods are in the same situation if, as you say, they quarrel about the just and unjust, and some say they wrong one another, and others deny this. For surely neither the gods nor man will ever try to say the doer of evil is not to be punished—you don't mean to tell me that?

EUTH: That is true, Socrates, in general.

SOC: But they disagree about particulars and this applies not only to men but also to the gods. If they disagree at all they disagree about some act which is called in question, and which some affirm to be just, others to be unjust. Is that true?

EUTH: Quite true.

SOC: Well then, my dear friend Euthyphro, do tell me, for my instruction, what proof do you have that in the opinion of all the gods a servant who is guilty of murder, and is put in chains by the master of the dead man, and dies because he is put in chains before his corrector can learn from the authorities what he ought to do with him, dies unjustly; and that on behalf of him a son should proceed against his father and accuse his father of murder? How would you show that all the gods absolutely agree in approving of his act? Prove that to me and I will applaud your wisdom as long as you live.

EUTH: That would not be an easy task, although I could make the matter very clear to you.

SOC: I understand. You mean I am not so quick as the jury, for to them you will be sure to prove the act is unjust, and hateful to the gods.

EUTH: Yes indeed, Socrates, at least if they will listen to me.

SOC: They will be sure to listen if they find you are a good speaker. There was a notion that came into my mind while you were speaking. I said to myself: "Well, and what if Euthyphro does prove to me that all the gods regarded the death of the laborer as unjust, how do I know anything more of the nature of holy and unholy? Granting this action may be hateful to the gods, still these distinctions have no bearing on the definition of holy

Socrates' general point is

_____

_____

_____

_____

_____.

Find and underline the third definition of the holy.

and unholy, for that which is hateful to some of the gods has been shown to be also pleasing and dear to others." And therefore, Euthyphro, I don't ask you to prove this. I suppose, if you like, all the gods hate such an action. But I will change the definition to say that what *all* the gods hate is unholy, and what they *all* love is holy and what some of them love and others hate is both or neither. Shall this be our definition of holiness and unholiness?

EUTH: Why not, Socrates?

SOC: No reason as far as I am concerned, Euthyphro. But whether this admission will greatly assist you in instructing me as you promised is what you should consider.

EUTH: Yes, I would say what all the gods love is holy and the opposite, which they all hate, unholy.

SOC: Should we investigate into the truth of this, Euthyphro, or simply accept the mere statement on our own authority and that of others?

EUTH: We should investigate, and I believe the statement will stand the test of our investigation.

The next two pages are the most challenging in the *Euthyphro*. Read them several times and underline important points.

SOC: That, my good friend, we shall know better in a little while. The point which I want first to understand is whether the holy is loved by the gods because it is holy, or holy because it is loved by the gods.

EUTH: I don't understand your meaning, Socrates.

SOC: I will try to explain. We speak of carrying and we speak of something being carried, or leading and something being led, seeing and something being seen. And there is a difference which you understand.

EUTH: I think I understand.

SOC: And is something that is loved different from the one who does the loving?

EUTH: Certainly.

SOC: Well tell me, is what is carried in this condition of being carried because someone carries, or for some other reason?

EUTH: No, that is the reason.

SOC: And the same is true of what is led and of what is seen?

EUTH: True.

The major idea Socrates establishes
is _____
_____
_____
_____
_____
_____ .

SOC: And someone does not see an object because it is a seen object, it is a seen object because someone sees it. Someone does not lead an object because it is a led object, it is a led object because someone leads it. Something is a carried object because someone carries it, someone does not carry the object because it is a carried object. And now I think, Euthyphro, my meaning will be clear and my meaning is that any effect [like being carried] implies a previous cause [like someone carrying]. It is not an effect because it is an effect, but it is an effect because of a previous cause. It does not occur because it is in a state of occurring, but it is in a state of occurring because something caused it to occur. Do you admit that?

EUTH: Yes.

SOC: Is that which is loved either the cause or the effect of something else?

EUTH: Yes.

SOC: And the same holds as in the previous instances; the effect of something being loved follows the cause of someone loving it. The effect does not come before the cause.

EUTH: That is certain.

SOC: And what do you say of the holy, Euthyphro: Is the holy, according to your definition, loved by all the gods?

EUTH: Yes.

SOC: Because it is holy, or for some other reason?

EUTH: No, that is the reason.

SOC: It is loved because it is holy, not holy because it is loved?

EUTH: Yes.

SOC: And that which is loved by the gods is in a state of being loved by them because they love it.

EUTH: Certainly.

SOC: Then what is loved by the gods, Euthyphro, is not the same as the holy, nor is what is holy the same as what is loved by the gods, as you say. They are two different things.

EUTH: What do you mean, Socrates?

SOC: I mean the holy has been defined by us as loved by the gods because it is holy, not holy because it is loved.

EUTH: Yes.

SOC: But that which is defined as loved by the gods has that definition because the gods love it. They do not love something because they love it.

EUTH: True.

SOC: But, friend Euthyphro, if that which is holy is the same as that which is loved by the gods and that which is holy is loved because it is holy, then that which is loved by the gods would have been loved because it is loved by the gods; but if what is loved by the gods is loved by them because it is loved by them, then that which is holy would have been holy because it is loved by them. But now you see that the reverse is the case, and that they are quite different from one another. The one is loved because it is initially worthy of love, the other is worthy of love because it is initially loved. Thus you appear to me, Euthyphro, when I ask you what is the essence of holiness, to offer a characteristic only, and not the essence—the characteristic of being loved by all the gods. But you still refuse to explain to me the essence of the holy.

Socrates is saying _____
_____
_____
_____
_____ .

A good example would be _____
_____
_____
_____ .

Stop. There is nothing more difficult on our tour than the following paragraph. Be *very* patient. You will understand slightly more with each re-reading. For extra help, complete pages 25 to 27.

The basic idea of this paragraph
seems to be _____
_____
_____
_____
_____ .

Since the beginning of the
dialogue, Euthyphro's mood has
changed from _____
_____
to _____
_____ .

An example of the relationship
between the holy and the morally
right would be the relationship
between _____
and _____ .

And therefore, if you please, I will ask you not to hide your treasure but tell me once more what holiness really is, whether loved by the gods or not, for that is a matter about which we will not quarrel. And what is unholiness?

EUTH: I really do not know, Socrates, how to say what I mean. Somehow or other our arguments, on whatever ground we rest them, seem to walk away.

SOC: Your words, Euthyphro, are like the sculptures of my ancestor Daedalus.[5] If I were the creator of them, you might say this comes from my being his relation and this is the reason why my arguments walk away and won't remain fixed where they are placed. But now, as the words are your own, you must find some other complaint, for they certainly, as you yourself say, show an inclination to be on the move.

EUTH: No, Socrates, I still say you are the Daedalus who sets arguments in motion. I do not make them move for they would never have stirred, as far as I am concerned.

SOC: Then I must be greater than Daedalus. He only made his own inventions move, I move those of other people as well. And the wonder of it is, I would rather they did not. I would give the wisdom of Daedalus and the wealth of Tantalus to be able to hold them and keep them still.[6] But enough of this. As I see you are lazy, I will try to show you how you might teach me the nature of piety; and I hope that you will work harder. Tell me, then, is not that which is holy also morally right?

EUTH: Yes.

SOC: And is, then, all that is morally right also holy? Or, is that which is holy all morally right, but that which is morally right only in part, and not all, holy?

EUTH: I don't understand you, Socrates.

SOC: And yet I know you are as much wiser than I as you are younger. But, as I was saying, dear friend, the abundance of your wisdom makes you lazy. Please exert yourself, for there is no real difficulty in understanding me. What I mean I will explain by an illustration of what I do not mean. The poet (Stasinus) sings "Of Zeus, the author and creator of all these things, You will not tell: for where there is fear there is also reverence."[7]

I disagree with this poet. Shall I tell you why I disagree?

EUTH: Please do.

SOC: I would not say where there is fear there is also reverence. I am sure many persons fear poverty and disease, and similar evils, but I do not see they reverence what they fear.

EUTH: Very true.

SOC: But where reverence is, there is fear. He who has a feeling of reverence about any action also fears a bad reputation.

EUTH: No doubt.

SOC: Then are we wrong in saying where there is fear there is also reverence? No, there is not always reverence where there is fear; for fear is a more extended concept, and reverence is a part of fear, just as the odd is a part of number, and number is a more extended concept than the odd. I suppose you follow me now?

EUTH: Quite well.

SOC: That was the sort of question I meant to raise when asking whether the morally right is the holy, or the holy the morally right; and whether there may be moral rightness where there is no holiness; for moral rightness is the larger concept of which the holy is only a part. Do you agree in that?

EUTH: Yes, that, I think, is correct.

SOC: Then if holiness is a part of moral rightness, I suppose we should inquire what part? If you had asked me what is an even number, and what part of number the even is, I should have had no difficulty in replying, a number which can be divided into two equal whole numbers. Do you agree?

EUTH: Yes.

SOC: In the same way, I want you to tell me what part of the morally right is the holy. Thus, will I be able to tell Meletus not to do me injustice, or indict me for impiety, as I am now adequately instructed by you in the nature of holiness and its opposites.

EUTH: The holy, Socrates, appears to me to be the part of moral rightness which attends to the gods, as there is the other part of moral rightness which attends to men.

SOC: That is good, Euthyphro; yet still there is a little point about which I would like to have further information. What is the meaning of "attention?" For attention can hardly be used in the same sense when applied to the gods as when applied to other things. For instance, horses are said to require attention, and not every person is able to attend to them, but only a person skilled in horsemanship. Is that true?

EUTH: Quite true.

SOC: I suppose that the art of horsemanship is the art of attending to horses?

EUTH: Yes.

SOC: Nor is everyone qualified to attend to dogs, but only the huntsman.

EUTH: True.

SOC: And I would also think the art of the huntsman is the art of attending to dogs?

EUTH: Yes.

SOC: As the art of the oxherd is the art of attending to oxen?

EUTH: Very true.

SOC: And holiness is the art of attending to the gods—that would be your meaning, Euthyphro?

From this page until the end of the *Euthyphro*, underline each new definition of the holy and any other important points.

EUTH: Yes.

SOC: And is not attention always designed for the good or benefit of that to which the attention is given? As in the case of horses, you may observe that when attended to by the horseman's art they are benefited and improved, are they not?

EUTH: True.

SOC: As dogs are benefited by the huntsman's art, and oxen by the art of the oxherd, and all other things are tended or attended for their good and not for their harm?

EUTH: Certainly, not for their harm.

SOC: But for their good?

EUTH: Of course.

SOC: And does holiness, which was defined as the art of attending to the gods, benefit or improve them? Would you say when you do a holy act you make any of the gods better?

EUTH: No, no, that is certainly not my meaning.

SOC: Indeed, Euthyphro, I did not suppose this was your meaning. That was the reason I asked you the nature of this attention, because I thought this was not your meaning.

EUTH: Thank you, Socrates, for that is not what I meant.

SOC: Good, but I must still ask what is this attention to the gods which is called holiness?

EUTH: It is the same, Socrates, as servants give to their masters.

SOC: I understand—a sort of service to the gods.

EUTH: Exactly.

SOC: Medicine is also a kind of service to attain some goal. Would you not say the goal was health?

EUTH: Yes.

SOC: Again, there is an art of the shipbuilder with a specific goal?

EUTH: Yes, Socrates, the goal of building a ship.

SOC: As there is an art of the house-builder with the goal of building a house?

EUTH: Yes.

SOC: And now tell me, my good friend, about this art which serves the gods: What work does that help to accomplish? For you must surely know if, as you say, you are of all men living the one who is best instructed in religion.

EUTH: And that is true, Socrates.

SOC: Tell me then, oh tell me—what is the good work which the gods do by the help of us as their servants?

EUTH: Many, Socrates, are the works which they do.

SOC: Why, my friend, and so are those of a general. But the main one is easily described. Would you not say that victory in war is the main one?

EUTH: Certainly.

SOC: Many, too, are the works of the farmer, if I am not wrong; but his chief work is growing food.

By this point in the dialogue, the reader understands Euthyphro is the kind of person who _____ _____ _____ _____ _____ _____ .

EUTH: Exactly.

SOC: And of the many things which the gods do, which is the main one?

EUTH: I have told you already, Socrates, that to learn all these things accurately will be very tiresome. Let me simply say that holiness is learning how to please the gods in word and deed, by prayers and sacrifices. That is holiness, which is the salvation of families and states, just as unholiness, which is unpleasing to the gods, is their ruin and destruction.

SOC: I think you could have answered in many fewer words the main question I asked, Euthyphro, if you had chosen. But I see plainly you do not want to instruct me: Otherwise why, when we had reached the present point, did you turn aside? If you had only answered me, I would have learned from you by this time the nature of holiness. Now, as the asker of a question is necessarily dependent on the answerer, where you lead I must follow. I can only ask again, what is the holy, and what is holiness? Do you mean they are a sort of science of praying and sacrificing?

Socrates is the kind of person who

_____

_____

_____

_____

_____

_____

EUTH: Yes, I do.

SOC: And sacrificing is giving to the gods, and prayer is asking of the gods?

EUTH: Yes, Socrates.

SOC: According to this, then holiness is a science of asking and giving?

EUTH: You understand me perfectly, Socrates.

SOC: Yes, my friend, the reason is I am a follower of your science, and give my mind to it, and therefore nothing which you say will be thrown away. Please then tell me, what is the nature of this service to the gods? Do you mean that we make requests and give gifts to them?

EUTH: Yes, I do.

SOC: Is not the right way of asking to ask of them what we want?

EUTH: Certainly.

SOC: And the right way of giving is to give to them in return what they want from us. There would be no meaning in an art which gives to any one what he does not want.

EUTH: Very true, Socrates.

SOC: Then holiness, Euthyphro, is an art which gods and men have of doing business with one another?

EUTH: That is an expression which you may use, if you like.

SOC: But I have no particular liking for anything but the truth. I wish, however, you would tell me what benefit comes to the gods from our gifts. That they are the givers of every good to us is clear; but how we can give any good thing to them in return is far from being equally clear. If they give everything and we give nothing, that must be an affair of business in which we have a great advantage over them.

EUTH: And do you imagine, Socrates, that any benefit comes to the gods from what they receive from us?

SOC: But if not, Euthyphro, what sort of gifts do we give the gods?

EUTH: What should we give them, but tributes of honor and, as I was just now saying, what is pleasing to them?

SOC: Holiness, then, is pleasing to the gods, but not beneficial or dear to them?

EUTH: I should say that nothing could be dearer.

SOC: Then once more the assertion is repeated that holiness is dear to the gods?

EUTH: No doubt.

SOC: And when you say this, can you wonder at your words not standing firm, but walking away? Will you accuse me of being the Daedalus who makes them walk away, not seeing there is another and far greater artist than Daedalus who makes them go round in a circle and that is yourself. For, the argument, as you will see, comes round to the same point. I think you must remember our saying the holy was not the same as that which is loved by the gods. Do you remember that?

EUTH: I do.

SOC: And do you not see what is loved of the gods is the holy and this is the same as what is dear to them?

EUTH: True.

SOC: Then either we were wrong before, or, if we were right then, we are wrong now.

EUTH: I suppose that is the case.

SOC: Then we must begin again and ask, what is holiness? That is an inquiry which I shall never be tired of pursuing as far as I can. I beg you not to reject me, but to apply your mind to the utmost and tell me the truth. For, if any man knows, you are the one and therefore I shall hold you, like Proteus, until you tell me. For if you had not known the nature of holiness and unholiness, I am confident you would never have, on behalf of a laborer, charged your aged father with murder. You would not have run such a risk of doing wrong in the sight of the gods and you would have had too much respect for the opinions of men. I am sure, therefore, you know the nature of holiness and unholiness. Speak out then, my dear Euthyphro, and do not hide your knowledge.

EUTH: Another time, Socrates, for I am in a hurry and must go now.

SOC: Alas! My companion, will you leave me in despair? I was hoping you would instruct me in the nature of holiness and unholiness, so I might have cleared myself of Meletus and his indictment. Then I might have proved to him I had been converted by Euthyphro and had given up rash innovations and

What has happened to Euthyphro

is _____

_____

_____

_____

_____

_____

_____ .

speculations, in which I had indulged through ignorance, and was about to lead a better life.

Thinking about the Euthyphro

(Note to the teacher: Sections of the following questions are numbered to facilitate assignments and discussion.)

Respond to the following questions in the spaces provided.

1. Perhaps this is the first piece of philosophy you have ever read. Why do you think Plato wrote it?

Perhaps because _____

_____

_____

_____

_____ or because _____

_____

_____

_____

_____. My main reaction was _____

_____

_____

_____

_____ .

What kind of person is Socrates?

If I had to pick three characteristics, I would say he is _____

_____

_____ because _____

_____

_____ and he is _____

_____

_____ because _____

_____

_____. He also is _____

_____

_____ because _____

_____

_____.

How about Euthyphro?

Euthyphro's three main characteristics and one good example

of each are _____

_____

_____

_____

_____

_____

_____

_____.

2. How many different definitions of holiness did you find?

I think there are _____. The first one, of course, is _____

_____

_____

_____. The others, in order, are _____

_____

_____

_____

_____

_____

_____

_____

_____

_____.

3. Now, let us consider two of Socrates' refutations in more
detail. Euthyphro's first definition of the holy is that holiness

is the act of prosecuting his father for murder. How does Socrates show Euthyphro this is wrong?

Socrates argues this is not a definition of holiness because

_____

_____

_____

_____

_____ . If asked to define a car, an example of Euthyphro's kind of error would be to say that a car is _____

_____

_____

_____ . In fact, a real definition of a car would involve _____

_____

_____

_____

_____ .

In the refutation of the third definition of the holy, Socrates states "Someone does not see an object because it is a seen object, it is a seen object because someone sees it. Someone does not lead an object because it is a led object, it is a led object because someone leads it." This may not be simple to understand. Think of your own example and try to explain his point.

One example of what Socrates is saying would be _____

_____

_____

_____

_____ . The point he is trying to make is _____

_____

_____

_____

_____

_____.

Later in this refutation, Socrates asks Euthyphro if (a) the gods love something because it is holy or (b) something is holy because the gods love it. Let us say you make a holy prayer to get a good grade in philosophy. In the case of (a), which comes first—the holiness of your prayer or the gods loving it?

I would say _____ comes first in the case of (a), because

_____

_____

_____.

Let's try that one more time. In the case of (a) is your prayer holy and then the gods love it, or does the prayer become holy because the gods love it?

I would say _____

_____

_____ because _____

_____

_____.

Now, from the point of view of statement (b), which comes first—the holiness of the prayer or the gods' love of it?

I would say _____

_____

_____ because _____

_____

_____

_____ .

Which comes first, cause or effect?

_____ always comes before _____ .

What is the cause and effect in statement (a)? In statement (b)?

In (a) the cause is _____

_____ and the effect is _____

_____ . In (b) the cause is

_____ and the effect is _____

_____ .

Which of the two does Euthyphro choose, (a) or (b)?

Looking back in the text, I see Euthyphro chooses _____

as a definition of holiness. This cannot be a definition of the

holy because _____

_____

_____

_____

_____

_____ .

4. Of all the definitions of the holy, which do you think is closest
to the truth?

The best definition is probably _____

_____

_____

_____

_____

_____ .

Now, try your own hand at thinking about the holy. Let us
say we both agree that Mother Teresa of India is holy. She lives
in poverty, helps the poorest of the poor, and has no concern for

herself. And let us assume that God loves her. Does God's love make her holy, or is she holy and God loves her as a result?

I would say _____

_____

_____ because _____

_____

_____

_____ .

Take this another step. Let us say you perform the good action of sending money to Mother Teresa. Is this a good action because God loves such actions, or is it good all by itself? Does the goodness come from the action or from God's approval? If you take the coward's way out and say "both," then tell me the difference between the goodness that comes from sending money and the goodness that comes from God.

I would say that the act of sending money _____

_____

_____

_____

_____

_____

_____ .

5. See if you can do better than Euthyphro in defining the holy. Here are three actions, which we will assume are holy: giving money to the poor, going to church regularly, and loving your enemies. A definition of the holy would show what all these actions have in common. What do you say holiness is?

Several possible definitions occur to me. One thing these actions have in common is _____

_____

_____ . Thus, holiness might be _____

_____

_____

_____

_____

_____. Another thing these actions

have in common is _____

_____

_____. Therefore holiness would be

_____

_____

_____

_____

_____. Finally, my own view is that

the holy is _____

_____

_____

_____

_____

_____. However, a possible

criticism of this might be that _____

_____

_____

_____

_____

Welcome to philosophy.

Euthyphro *Quiz*

The following quiz is, obviously, open book. I've mixed up easy with challenging questions.

1. Euthyphro's first definition of the holy is: (exact quote): "_

_____

_____"

In his first definition, Euthyphro confuses a definition with an example. Review pages 12–13 and then answer the following.

2. T or F: From Socrates' point of view, examples are more general than definitions.

3. T or F: It would be consistent with Socrates' point of view to say that a mammal is an example of a dog.

4. T or F: Defining a flower as a rose would be an example of Euthyphro's kind of error.

5. T or F: Defining freedom as the rights given to Americans in the Bill of Rights would be an example of Euthyphro's kind of error.

6. The second definition of the holy is: (exact quote): "_____

_____

_____."

Socrates' refutation of Euthyphro's second definition involves a distinction between two kinds of disagreements. Carefully review what Socrates says on pages 13–16 about the kinds of issues the gods can and cannot agree upon. Which of the following statements are generally consistent (C) or generally inconsistent (I) with Socrates' position?

7. C or I: Zeus and Hera will never be able to agree about the distance between Athens and Sparta.

8. C or I: Apollo and Dionysus will be able to agree on the number of steps leading to the Parthenon.

9. C or I: If Aphrodite and Demeter disagree about the nature of Love, they may not be able to resolve their disagreements.

10. C or I: If Athena loves Euthyphro and finds him righteous and Zeus hates Euthyphro and finds him unrighteous, then it is correct to say that Euthyphro is both righteous and unrighteous.

11. C or I: Because the gods may disagree on moral issues, there is no absolute right and wrong.

12. The third definition of the holy is (exact quote): "_____

_____

_____."

After the third definition of the holy, Socrates makes a distinction between (a) something being holy because the gods love it and (b) the gods loving something because it is holy.

13. T or F: In the case of (a), the gods' love is the effect of something being holy.

14. T or F: In the case of (b), the gods' love is the cause of something being holy.

15. T or F: In the case of (a), the gods' love is the essence of the holy.

16. T or F: In the case of (b), the gods' love is a nonessential characteristic of the holy.

17. T or F: In the case of (a), the gods are so powerful that whatever they love becomes holy.

18. T or F: In the case of (b), the gods are so weak that even if they hate something, it does not become unholy.

19. T or F: In the case of (a), the gods' love is to the holy as circularity is to circle. (In other words, you can't have the holy without the gods' love, just as you can't have a circle without circularity.)

20. T or F: In the case of (b), the gods' love is to the holy as "Presidentialness" is to Bill Clinton.

21. T or F: In the case of (a), the gods' love is to the holy as "Presidentialness" is to the president.

Socrates presents a complex refutation of the third definition. Which of the following statements are generally consistent (C) or generally inconsistent (I) with Socrates' refutation?

22. C or I: A seen object is to the one who sees it as cause is to effect.

23. C or I: To say that the gods' love is the result of something's holiness is to describe the holy in terms of what is nonessential rather than what is essential.

24. C or I: To say the gods' love is the cause of an action's holiness is more like a definition than to say the gods' love is the effect of an action's holiness.

25. C or I: The gods will never agree on what is holy.

26. C or I: The holy is a kind of trading skill between the gods and men.

27. The fourth definition of the holy is: (exact quote): "_____

_____

_____."

Socrates makes a point about the relationship between the holy and the morally right. Decide which of the following analogies are True (accurate analogies) or False (inaccurate analogies).

28. T or F: The holy is to the morally right as cat is to dog.

29. T or F: The holy is to the morally right as orange is to fruit.

30. T or F: The holy is to the morally right as the United States is to Missouri.

31. T or F: The holy is to the morally right as 1 is to the set of all numbers.

32. T or F: The holy is to the morally right as cow is to mammal.

33. T or F: The holy is to the morally right as Bob Dylan is to singers.

34. T or F: The holy is to the morally right as world capitals are to Athens.

35. T or F: The holy is to the morally right as high is to low.

36. T or F: The holy is to the morally right as the morally right is to the holy.

Vote and Debate

Your teacher may decide to use the following to prompt a class discussion. Cast your vote, Agree or Disagree, on each of the following assertions and then write down evidence to back up your position.

1. Socrates plays mind games.

Agree _____ Disagree _____ Evidence: _____

_____

_____

_____ .

2. Holiness has no universal essence. What is holy for one person would be unholy to another.

Agree _____ Disagree _____ Evidence: _____

_____

_____

_____ .

3. Euthyphro is a bad person.

Agree _____ Disagree _____ Evidence: _____

_____

_____

4. Because the dialogue does not define the holy, Plato accomplished nothing writing the *Euthyphro*.

Agree _____ Disagree _____ Evidence: _____

_____

_____

_____ .

5. Euthyphro would make a better roommate than Socrates.

Agree _____ Disagree _____ Evidence: _____

_____

_____

_____ .

/2/ *APOLOGY*

rational defense

Preview

In this dialogue Socrates is in court and offers not an "apology," but a defense. The Athenian jury in this case consists of 501 citizens. It was the custom for each side to present its case and then, if the defendant was found guilty, each side would propose a punishment. The jury would then choose between the proposed punishments.

Annotation Tasks

Background Information. The *Apology* contains a considerable amount of information about Socrates' life. Confine your attention in the first few pages to finding the two groups of accusers and the charges against him.

Main Theme. The theme is simply Socrates' defense. First, look for the main points he makes against his accusers, and then look for the points he makes after hearing the jury's verdict.

Apology

SOCRATES: How you have felt, O men of Athens, hearing the speeches of my accusers, I cannot tell. I know their persuasive words almost made me forget who I was, such was their effect. Yet they hardly spoke a word of truth. But many as their falsehoods were, there was one of them which quite amazed me—I mean when they told you to be on your guard and not let yourselves be deceived by the force of my eloquence. They ought to have been ashamed of saying this, because they were sure to be detected as soon as I opened my lips and displayed my deficiency. They certainly did appear to be most shameless in saying this, unless by the force of eloquence they mean the force of truth; for then I do indeed admit that I am eloquent. But in how different a way from theirs!

According to Socrates, the difference between him and his accusers is _____ _____ _____ _____ _____ _____ .

Well, as I was saying, they have hardly uttered a word, or not more than a word, of truth. You shall hear from me the whole truth: not, however, delivered in their manner, in an oration ornamented with words and phrases. No, indeed! I shall use the words and arguments which occur to me at the moment. I am certain this is right, and at my time of life I should not appear before you, O men of Athens, in the character of a juvenile orator—let no one expect this of me. And I must beg you to grant me one favor, which is this—if you hear me using the same words in my defense which I have been in the habit of using, and which most of you may have heard in the agora, and at the tables of the money-changers, or anywhere else, I ask you not to be surprised at this, and not to interrupt me. I am more than 70 years of age and this is the first time I have ever appeared in a court of law, and I am a stranger to the ways of this place. Therefore I would have you regard me as if I were really a stranger whom you would excuse if he spoke in his native tongue and after the fashion of his country. That, I think, is not an unfair request. Never mind the way I speak, which may or may not be good, but think only of the justice of my cause, and give heed to that. Let the judge decide justly and the speaker speak truly.

First, I have to reply to the older charges and to my first accusers, and then I will go on to the later ones. I have had many accusers who accused me in the past, and their false charges have continued during many years. I am more afraid of them than of Anytus and his associates, who are dangerous, too, in their own way. But far more dangerous are these, who began when you were children and took possession of your minds with their falsehoods, telling of Socrates, a wise man, who speculated about the heavens above, and searched into the earth beneath, and made the worse argument defeat the better. These are the accusers whom I fear because they are the circulators of this rumor and their listeners are too likely to believe that speculators of this sort do not believe in the gods. My accusers are many and their charges against me are of ancient date. They made them in days when you were impressionable—in childhood, or perhaps in youth—and the charges went by unanswered for there was none to answer. Hardest of all, their names I do not know and cannot tell, unless in the chance case of a comic poet.[1] But the main body of these slanderers who

The hardest group of accusers to refute is _____ because _____ _____ _____ _____ _____ .

from envy and malice have convinced you—and there are some of them who are convinced themselves, and impart their convictions to others—all these, I say, are most difficult to deal with. I cannot have them up here and examine them. Therefore, I must simply fight with shadows in my own defense and examine when there is no one who answers. I will ask you then to assume with me that my opponents are of two kinds: one more recent, the other from the past. I will answer the latter first, for these accusations you heard long before the others, and much more often.

Well, then, I will make my defense, and I will try in the short time allowed to do away with this evil opinion of me which you have held for such a long time. I hope I may succeed, if this be well for you and me, and that my words may find favor with you. But I know to accomplish this is not easy—I see the nature of the task. Let the event be as the gods will; in obedience to the law I make my defense.

I will begin at the beginning and ask what the accusation is which has given rise to this slander of me and which has encouraged Meletus to proceed against me. What do the slanderers say? They shall be my prosecutors and I will sum up their words in an affidavit. "Socrates is an evil-doer and a curious person, who searches into things under the earth and in the heavens. He makes the weaker argument defeat the stronger and he teaches these doctrines to others." That is the nature of the accusation and that is what you have seen in the comedy of Aristophanes. He introduced a man whom he calls Socrates, going about and saying he can walk in the air and talking a lot of nonsense concerning matters which I do not pretend to know anything about—however, I mean to say nothing disparaging of anyone who is a student of such knowledge. I should be very sorry if Meletus could add that to my charge. But the simple truth is, O Athenians, I have nothing to do with these studies. Very many of those here are witnesses to the truth of this and to them I appeal. Speak then, you who have heard me, and tell your neighbors whether any of you ever heard me hold forth in few words or in many upon matters of this sort. . . . You hear their answer. And from what they say you will be able to judge the truth of the rest.

There is the same foundation for the report I am a teacher and take money; that is no more true than the other. Although, if a man is able to teach, I honor him for being paid. There are Gorgias of Leontium, Prodicus of Ceos, and Hippias of Elis,[2] who go round the cities and are able to persuade young men to leave their own citizens, by whom they might be taught for nothing, and come to them, whom they not only pay but are also thankful if they may be allowed to pay them.

Underline these charges and note how Socrates refers to them later.

The main points Socrates has made thus far are _____
_____
_____
_____
_____
_____ .

There is actually a Parian philosopher residing in Athens who charges fees. I came to hear of him in this way: I met a man who spent a world of money on the sophists, Callias, the son of Hipponicus, and knowing he had sons, I asked him: "Callias," I said, "if your two sons were foals or calves, there would be no difficulty in finding someone to raise them. We would hire a trainer of horses, or a farmer probably, who would improve and perfect them in their own proper virtue and excellence. But, as they are human beings, whom are you thinking of placing over them? Is there anyone who understands human and political virtue? You must have thought about this because you have sons. Is there anyone?"

"There is," he said.

"Who is he?" said I. "And of what country? And what does he charge?"

"Evenus the Parian,"[3] he replied. "He is the man and his charge is five minae."

Happy is Evenus, I said to myself, if he really has this wisdom and teaches at such a modest charge. Had I the same, I would have been very proud and conceited; but the truth is I have no knowledge like this, O Athenians.

I am sure someone will ask the question, "Why is this, Socrates, and what is the origin of these accusations of you; for there must have been something strange which you have been doing? All this great fame and talk about you would never have come up if you had been like other men. Tell us then, why this is, as we should be sorry to judge you too quickly."

I regard this as a fair challenge, and I will try to explain to you the origin of this name of "wise" and of this evil fame. Please attend then and although some of you may think I am joking, I declare I will tell you the entire truth. Men of Athens, this reputation of mine has come from a certain kind of wisdom which I possess. If you ask me what kind of wisdom, I reply, such wisdom as is attainable by man, for to that extent I am inclined to believe I am wise. Whereas the persons of whom I was speaking have a superhuman wisdom which I may fail to describe, because I do not have it. He who says I have, speaks false and slanders me.

O men of Athens, I must beg you not to interrupt me, even if I seem to say something extravagant. For the word which I will speak is not mine. I will refer you to a wisdom which is worthy of credit and will tell you about my wisdom—whether I have any and of what sort—and that witness shall be the god of Delphi.[4] You must have known Chaerephon. He was a friend of mine and also a friend of yours, for he shared in the exile of the people and returned with you. Well, Chaerephon, as you know, was very impetuous in all his doings, and he went to Delphi and boldly

Socrates' ironic point about

Evenus is _____

_____

_____

_____

_____ .

Underline on this and on the next two pages the main points Socrates makes about his experience with the oracle at Delphi.

asked the oracle to tell him whether—as I said, I must beg you not to interrupt—he asked the oracle to tell him whether there was anyone wiser than I was. The Pythian prophetess answered, there was no man wiser. Chaerephon is dead himself but his brother, who is in court, will confirm the truth of this story.

Why do I mention this? Because I am going to explain to you why I have such an evil name. When I heard the answer, I said to myself, "What can the god mean and what is the interpretation of this riddle? I know I have no wisdom, great or small. What can he mean when he says I am the wisest of men? And yet he is a god and cannot lie; that would be against his nature." After long consideration, I at last thought of a method of answering the question.

Socrates' plan is to _____
_____
_____
because _____
_____
_____
_____ .

I reflected if I could only find a man wiser than myself, then I might go to the god with a refutation in my hand. I would say to him, "Here is a man who is wiser than I am, but you said I was the wisest." Accordingly I went to one who had the reputation of wisdom and observed him—his name I need not mention; he was a politician whom I selected for examination. When I began to talk with him I could not help thinking he was not really wise, although he was thought wise by many and wiser still by himself. I tried to explain to him that he thought himself wise but was not really wise. The result was he hated me, and his hatred was shared by several who were present and heard me. So I left him, saying to myself, as I went away: "Well, although I do not suppose either of us knows anything really beautiful and good, I am better off than he is—for he knows nothing and thinks that he knows. I neither know nor think that I know. In this latter, then, I seem to have an advantage over him." Then I went to another who had still higher philosophical pretensions, and my conclusion was exactly the same. I made another enemy of him and of many others besides him.

After this I went to one man after another, being aware of the anger that I provoked; and I lamented and feared this, but necessity was laid upon me. The word of the god, I thought, ought to be considered first. And I said to myself, "I must go to all who appear to know and find out the meaning of the oracle." And I swear to you Athenians, by the dog, I swear,[5] the result of my mission was this: I found the men with the highest reputations were all nearly the most foolish and some inferior men were really wiser and better.

I will tell you the tale of my wanderings and of the Herculean labors,[6] as I may call them, which I endured only to find at last the oracle was right. When I left the politicians, I went to the poets: tragic, dithyrambic, and all sorts. There, I said to myself, you will be detected. Now you will find out you are more ignorant than they are. Accordingly, I took them some of the most elaborate passages in their own writings and asked what was the meaning of them—thinking the poets would teach me something. Will you believe me? I am almost ashamed to say this, but I must say there is hardly a person present who would not have talked better about their poetry than the poets did themselves. That quickly showed me poets do not write poetry by wisdom, but by a sort of inspiration. They are like soothsayers who also say many fine things, but do not understand the meaning of what they say. The poets appeared to me to be much the same, and I further observed that upon the strength of their poetry they believed themselves to be the wisest of men in other things in which they were not wise. So I departed, conceiving myself to be superior to them for the same reason I was superior to the politicians.

The ironies of Socrates' search are: _____ _____ _____ _____ .

At last I went to the artisans, because I was conscious I knew nothing at all, and I was sure they knew many fine things. In this I was not mistaken, for they did know many things of which I was ignorant, and in this they certainly were wiser than I was. But I observed even the good artisans fell into the same error as the poets. Because they were good workmen, they thought they also knew all sorts of high matters, and this defect in them over-shadowed their wisdom. Therefore, I asked myself on behalf of the oracle whether I would like to be as I was, having neither their knowledge nor their ignorance, or like them in both. I answered myself and the oracle that I was better off as I was.

The major groups Socrates visited were _____ _____ _____ .

This investigation led to my having many enemies of the worst and most dangerous kind and has given rise also to many false-hoods. I am called wise because my listeners always imagine I possess the wisdom which I do not find in others. The truth is, O men of Athens, the gods only are wise and in this oracle they mean to say wisdom of men is little or nothing. They are not speaking of Socrates, only using my name as an illustration, as if they said, "He, O men, is the wisest who, like Socrates, knows his wisdom is in truth worth nothing." And so I go my way, obedient to the gods, and seek wisdom of anyone, whether citizen or stranger, who appears to be wise. If he is not wise, then in support of the oracle I show him he is not wise. This occupation quite absorbs me, and I have no time to give either to any public matter of interest or to any concern of my own, but I am in utter poverty by reason of my devotion to the gods.

The important points established by this story are: _____ _____ _____ _____ _____ _____ .

There is another thing. Young men of the richer classes, who have little to do, gather around me of their own accord. They like to hear the pretenders examined. They often imitate me and examine others themselves. There are plenty of persons, as they soon enough discover, who think they know something, but really know little or nothing. Then those who are examined by the young men, instead of being angry with themselves, are angry with me. "This confounded Socrates," they say, "this villainous misleader of youth!" Then if somebody asks them, "Why, what evil does he practice or teach?," they do not know and cannot tell. But so they may not appear ignorant, they repeat the ready-made charges which are used against all philosophers about teaching things up in the clouds and under the earth, and having no gods, and making the worse argument defeat the stronger. They do not like to confess their pretense to knowledge has been detected, which it has. They are numerous, ambitious, energetic and are all in battle array and have persuasive tongues. They have filled your ears with their loud and determined slanders. This is the reason why my three accusers, Meletus and Anytus and Lycon, have set upon me. Meletus has a quarrel with me on behalf of the poets, Anytus, on behalf of the craftsmen, Lycon, on behalf of the orators. As I said at the beginning, I cannot expect to get rid of this mass of slander all in a moment.

This, O men of Athens, is the truth and the whole truth. I have concealed nothing. And yet I know this plainness of speech makes my accusers hate me, and what is their hatred but a proof that I am speaking the truth? This is the reason for their slander of me, as you will find out either in this or in any future inquiry.

Socrates' main defense against his first class of accusers is _____ _____ _____ _____ _____ .

I have said enough in my defense against the first class of my accusers. I turn to the second class who are headed by Meletus, that good and patriotic man, as he calls himself. Now I will try to defend myself against them: These new accusers must also have their affidavit read. What do they say? Something of this sort: "Socrates is a doer of evil and corrupter of the youth, and he does not believe in the gods of the state. He has other new divinities of his own." That is their charge and now let us examine the particular counts. He says I am a doer of evil who corrupts the youth, but I say, O men of Athens, Meletus is a doer of evil, and the evil is that he makes a joke of a serious matter. He is too ready to bring other men to trial from a pretended zeal and interest about matters in which he really never had the smallest interest. And the truth of this I will try to prove to you.

Come here, Meletus, and let me ask a question of you. You think a great deal about the improvement of youth?

Underline on this and the next three pages Socrates' main points in his examination of Meletus.

MELETUS: Yes I do.

SOCRATES: Tell the judges, then, who is their improver. You must know, as you have taken the pains to discover their corruptor and are accusing me before them. Speak then, and tell the judges who their improver is. Observe, Meletus, that you are silent and have nothing to say. But is this not rather disgraceful and a very great proof of what I was saying, that you have no interest in the matter? Speak up, friend, and tell us who their improver is.

MEL: The laws.

SOC: But that, my good sir, is not my meaning. I want to know who the person is, who, in the first place, knows the laws.

MEL: The jury, Socrates, who are present in court.

SOC: Do you mean to say Meletus, they are able to instruct and improve youth?

MEL: Certainly they are.

SOC: All of them, or only some and not others?

MEL: All of them.

SOC: By the goddess Hera, that is good news! There are plenty of improvers, then. And what do you say of the audience—do they improve them?

MEL: Yes, they do.

SOC: And the senators?

MEL: Yes, the senators improve them.

SOC: But perhaps the members of the Assembly corrupt them? Or do they too improve them?

MEL: They improve them.

SOC: Then every Athenian improves and elevates them, all with the exception of myself. I alone am their corruptor? Is that what you say?

MEL: Most definitely.

SOC: I am very unfortunate if that is true. But suppose I ask you a question. Would you say that this also holds true in the case of horses? Does one man do them harm and everyone else good? Is not the exact opposite of this true? One man is able to do them good and not the many. The trainer of horses, that is to say, does them good, and others who deal with horses injure them? Is that not true, Meletus, of horses or any other animals? Yes, certainly. Whether you and Anytus say yes or no, that is no matter. Fortunate indeed would be the condition of youth if they had one corruptor only and all the rest of the world were their improvers. You, Meletus, have sufficiently shown you never had a thought about the young. Your carelessness is seen in your not caring about the matters spoken of in this very indictment.

And now, Meletus, I must ask you another question: Which is better, to live among bad citizens or among good ones? Answer, friend, I say, for that is a question which may be easily answered. Do not the good do their neighbors good and the bad do them evil?

MEL: Certainly.

SOC: And is there anyone who would rather be injured than benefited by those who associate with him? Answer, my good friend, the law requires you to answer—does anyone like to be injured?

MEL: Certainly not.

SOC: And when you accuse me of corrupting the youth, do you charge I corrupt them intentionally or unintentionally?

The horse trainer is to horses

as _a _____

_____ is

to _____

_____ .

Thus, Socrates is arguing that _____

_____

_____

_____ .

MEL: Intentionally, I say.

SOC: But you just admitted that the good do their neighbors good, and the evil do them evil. Now, is that a truth which your superior wisdom has recognized thus early in life, and am I, at my age, in such ignorance as not to know if a man with whom I associate is corrupted by me, I am very likely to be harmed by him? Yet you say I corrupt him and intentionally too; of that you will never persuade me or any other human being. But either I do not corrupt them, or I corrupt them unintentionally, so that on either view of the case you lie. If my offense is unintentional, the law does not mention unintentional offenses. You ought to have taken me aside and warned me, because if I had been better advised, I should have stopped doing what I only did unintentionally—no doubt I should. Instead, you hated to talk with me or teach me and you indicted me in this court, which is a place not of instruction, but of punishment.

The key ideas in this paragraph

are ———————————

———————————

———————————

———————————

——————————— .

I have shown, Athenians, as I was saying, Meletus has no care at all, great or small, about the matter. But still I should like to know, Meletus, in what way do I corrupt the young? I suppose you mean, as I infer from your indictment, I teach them not to acknowledge the gods which the state acknowledges, but some other new divinities or spiritual agencies instead. These are the lessons which corrupt the youth, as you say.

MEL: Yes, I say that emphatically.

SOC: Then, by the gods, Meletus, of whom we are speaking, tell me and the court, in somewhat plainer terms, what you mean! I do not understand whether you charge I teach others to acknowledge some gods, and therefore do believe in gods, and am not an entire atheist—but only that they are not the same gods which the city recognizes—or, do you mean to say that I am an atheist simply, and a teacher of atheism?

MEL: I mean the latter—that you are a complete atheist.

SOC: That is an extraordinary statement, Meletus. Why do you say that? Do you mean that I do not believe the sun or moon are gods, which is the common belief of all men?

MEL: I assure you, jurymen, he does not believe in them. He says the sun is stone and the moon, earth.

SOC: Friend Meletus, you think you are accusing Anaxagoras[7] and you have a bad opinion of the jury, if you believe they do not know these doctrines are found in the books of Anaxagoras the Clazomenian. These are the doctrines which the youth are said to learn from Socrates, when these doctrines can be bought in the marketplace. The youth might cheaply purchase them and laugh at Socrates if he pretends to father such eccentricities. And so, Meletus, you really think that I do not believe in any god?

MEL: I swear by Zeus that you absolutely believe in none at all.

SOC: You are a liar, Meletus, not believed even by yourself. I cannot help thinking, O men of Athens, Meletus is reckless and impudent and has written this indictment in a spirit of wantonness and youthful bravado. He has made a riddle, thinking to fool me. He said to himself: "I shall see whether this wise Socrates will discover my ingenious contradiction, or whether I shall be able to deceive him and the rest of them." For he certainly does appear to me to contradict himself in the indictment as much as if he said that Socrates is guilty of not believing in the gods, and yet of believing in them—but this surely is a piece of nonsense.

I should like you, O men of Athens, to join me in examining what I conceive to be his inconsistency and you, Meletus, answer. And I must remind you not to interrupt me if I speak in my accustomed manner.

Did any man, Meletus, ever believe in the existence of human things and not human beings? . . . I wish, men of Athens, that he would answer and not be always trying to create an interruption. Did ever any man believe in horsemanship and not in horses? Or in flute playing and not in flute players? No, my friend, I will answer for you and to the court, as you refuse to answer for yourself. There is no man who ever did. But now, please answer the next question. Can a man believe in spiritual and divine activities and not in divine beings?

MEL: He cannot.

SOC: I am glad I have extracted that answer, by the assistance of the court. Nevertheless you swear in the indictment that I teach and believe in divine activities (new or old, no matter for that). At any rate, I believe in divine activities, as you swear in the affidavit, but if I believe in divine activities, I must believe in divine beings. Is that not true? Yes, that is true, for I may assume that your silence gives assent to that. Now what are divine beings? Are they not either gods or the sons of gods? Is that true?

MEL: Yes, that is true.

SOC: But this is just the ingenious riddle of which I was speaking. The divine beings are gods and you say first that I don't believe in gods, and then again that I do believe in gods; that is, if I believe in divine beings. For if the divine beings are the illegitimate sons of gods, whether by the nymphs or by any other mothers, as is thought, that, as all men will agree, necessarily implies the existence of their parents. You might as well affirm the existence of mules, and deny the existence of horses and donkeys. Such nonsense, Meletus, could only have been intended by you as a test of me. You have put this into the indictment because you had no real charge against me. But no one who has

Meletus' contradiction is _____
_____
_____ .
_____
_____ .

a particle of understanding will ever be convinced by you that the same men can believe in divine and superhuman activities and yet not believe that there are gods and demigods.

I have said enough in answer to the charge of Meletus. Any elaborate defense is unnecessary but, as I was saying before, I certainly have many enemies and this will be my destruction if I am destroyed; of that I am certain—not Meletus, nor Anytus, but the envy and slander of the world, which has been the death of many good men and will probably be the death of many more. I will not be the last of them.

Someone will say: Are you not ashamed, Socrates, of a way of life which is likely to bring you to an untimely end? To him I answer: There you are mistaken. A man who is good for anything should not calculate the chance of living or dying. He should only consider whether in doing anything he is doing right or wrong and acting the part of a good man or of a bad. Whereas, according to your view, the heroes who fell at Troy were not good for much, and the son of Thetis above all,[8] who altogether despised danger in comparison with disgrace. His goddess mother said to him, in his eagerness to slay Hector, that if he avenged his companion Patroclus, and slew Hector, he would die himself.

"Fate," as she said, "waits upon you next after Hector."

He, hearing this, utterly despised danger and death, and instead of fearing them, feared rather to live in dishonor and not to avenge his friend.

"Let me die next," he replied, "and be avenged of my enemy, rather than stay here by the beaked ships to be mocked and a burden on the earth."

Had Achilles any thought of death and danger? For wherever a man's place is, whether the place which he has chosen or that in which he has been placed by a commander, there he should remain in the hour of danger. He should not consider death or anything else but only disgrace. And this, O men of Athens, is a true saying.

My conduct would be strange, O men of Athens, if I, who was ordered by the generals you chose to command me at Potidaea, Amphipolis, and Delium, remained where they placed me, like any other man facing death, should now when, as I believe, God orders me to fulfill the philosopher's mission of searching into myself and other men, desert my post through fear of death or any other fear. That would indeed be strange, and I might be justly arraigned in court for denying the existence of the gods, if I disobeyed the oracle because I was afraid of death. Then I should be supposing I was wise when I was not wise.

This fear of death is indeed the imitation of wisdom, and not real wisdom, being the appearance of knowing the unknown. No

Stop for a moment and think about what you have read. There have been three major sections in the *Apology* thus far: an introduction, an answer to the first group of accusers, and an answer to the second group. The most important points were: (1) _____

_____

_____

_____

(2) _____

_____

_____

_____

(3) _____

_____

_____

_____ .

In the rest of the *Apology,* draw a line across the page wherever you think a new section begins.

one knows whether death, which they in their fear believe to be the greatest evil, may not be the greatest good. Is there not here the pretense of knowledge, which is a disgraceful sort of ignorance? This is the point in which, as I think, I am superior to men in general and in which I might believe myself wiser than other men. Whereas I know little of the other world, I do not suppose that I know. But I do know that injustice and disobedience to a better, whether god or man, is evil and dishonorable, and I will never fear or avoid a possible good rather than a certain evil. Therefore if you let me go now, reject the advice of Anytus, who said if I were not put to death I should not have been prosecuted, and that if I escape now, your sons will all be utterly ruined by listening to my words. If you say to me, Socrates, this time we will not listen to Anytus and will let you off, but upon one condition, you are not to inquire and speculate in this way any more and if you are caught doing this again you shall die—if this was the condition on which you let me go, I would reply: Men of Athens, I honor and love you but I shall obey the god rather than you. While I have life and strength I shall never cease from practicing and teaching philosophy, exhorting anyone whom I meet in my usual way and convincing him, saying: O my friend, why do you, who are a citizen of the great and wise city of Athens, care so much about laying up the greatest amount of money, honor, and reputation, and so little about wisdom, truth, and the greatest improvement of the soul, which you never regard or heed at all? Are you not ashamed of this? If the person with whom I am arguing says: Yes, but I do care; I do not depart or let him go at once. I question, examine and cross-examine him, and if I think he has no virtue, but only says he has, I reproach him with undervaluing the greater, and overvaluing the lesser. This I would say to everyone I meet, young and old, citizen and alien, but especially to the citizens, inasmuch as they are my brethren. This is the command of the god, as I would have you know and I believe that to this day no greater good has ever happened in the state than my service to the god.

I do nothing but go about persuading you all, old and young alike, not to take thought of yourself or your properties, but to care about the improvement of your soul. I tell you virtue is not acquired with money, but that from virtue come money and every other good of man, public as well as private. This is my teaching, and if this is the doctrine which corrupts the young, my influence is certainly ruinous. If anyone says this is not my teaching, he is speaking a lie. Therefore, O men of Athens, I say to you, do as Anytus bids or not as Anytus bids, and either acquit me or not; but whatever you do, know that I shall never change my ways, not even if I have to die many times.

Socrates sees his mission as _____ _____ _____ _____ _____ _____.

Underline Socrates' analogy between himself and a gadfly.

Men of Athens, do not interrupt, but hear me. There was an agreement between us that you should hear me out. I think what I am going to say will do you good: For I have something more to say, which you may be inclined to interrupt but I ask you not to do this.

I want you to know if you kill someone like me, you will injure yourselves more than you will injure me. Meletus and Anytus will not injure me. They cannot because it is not possible that a bad man should injure someone better than himself. I do not deny he may, perhaps, kill him, or drive him into exile, or deprive him of civil rights. He may imagine, and others may imagine, he is doing him a great injury but I do not agree with him. The evil of doing as Anytus is doing—of unjustly taking away another man's life—is far greater.

Now, Athenians, I am not going to argue for my own sake, as you may think, but for yours, that you may not sin against the gods or lightly reject their favor by condemning me. If you kill me you will not easily find another like me, who, if I may use such a ludicrous figure of speech, am a sort of gadfly, given to the State by the gods. The State is like a great and noble steed who is slow in his motions owing to his very size and needs to be stirred into life. I am that gadfly which the gods have given the State and all day long and in all places am always fastening upon you, arousing, persuading, and reproaching you. As you will not easily find another like me, I would advise you to spare me. I believe you may feel irritated at being suddenly awakened when you are caught napping. You may think if you were to strike me dead, as Anytus advises, which you easily might, then you would sleep on for the remainder of your lives, unless the god in his care of you gives you another gadfly. That I am given to you by the god is proved by this: If I had been like other men, I should not have neglected my own concerns all these years, and been occupied with yours, coming to you individually like a father or elder brother, exhorting you to think about virtue. This, I say, would not be like human nature. If I had gained anything, or if my exhortations had been paid, there would be some sense in that; but now, as you see, not even my accusers dare to say I have ever sought pay from anyone. They have no witnesses for that. I have a witness of the truth of what I say; my poverty is my witness.

Someone may wonder why I go about in private giving advice and busying myself with the concerns of others, but do not come forward in public and advise the State. I will tell you the reason for this. You have often heard me speak of a spiritual sign which comes to me and is the divinity which Meletus ridicules in the indictment. This sign I have had ever since I was a child. The sign

Socrates' service to the State

is _____

_____

_____

_____ .

is a spiritual voice which comes to me and always forbids me to do something which I am going to do, but never commands me to do anything. This is what stands in the way of my being a politician. And correctly I think. For I am certain, O men of Athens, if I had engaged in politics, I would have perished long ago, and done no good either to you or to myself. Do not be offended at my telling you the truth. The truth is no man who goes to war with you or any other multitude, honestly struggling against acts of unrighteousness in the state, will save his life. He who will really fight for the right, if he would live even for a little while, must have a private station and not a public one.

Socrates did not become a politician because _____ _____ _____ _____ _____ .

I can give you proofs of this, not words only, but deeds, which you value more than words. Let me tell you a part of my own life which will prove to you I would never have yielded to injustice from any fear of death, and that in not yielding I should have died at once. I will tell you a story—tasteless perhaps and commonplace, but nevertheless true. . . .

The only office of state which I ever held, O men of Athens, was when I served on the council. The clan Antiochis, which is my clan, had the presidency at the trial of the generals who had not taken up the bodies of the slain after the battle of Arginusae. You proposed to try them all together, which was illegal, as you all thought afterward, but at the time I was the only one of the committee who was opposed to the illegality. I gave my vote against you. When the orators threatened to impeach and arrest me and have me taken away, and you called and shouted, I made up my mind I would run the risk, having law and justice with me, rather than take part in your injustice because I feared imprisonment and death. This happened in the days of the democracy. But when the oligarchy of the Thirty was in power, they brought me and four others into the rotunda, and told us to bring in Leon from Salamis because they wanted to execute him. This was an example of the sort of commands which they were always giving in order to implicate as many as possible in their crimes. Then I showed, not in word only but in deed, if I may be allowed to use such an expression, I cared not a straw for death, and my only fear was the fear of doing an unrighteous or unholy thing. The strong arm of that oppressive power did not frighten me into doing wrong. When we came out of the rotunda the other four went to Salamis and fetched Leon, but I went quietly home. For this I might have lost my life, had not the power of the Thirty shortly afterward come to an end. And to this many will witness.

The point of this story about the Thirty is _____ _____ _____ _____ .

Now do you really imagine I could have survived all these years if I had led a public life, supposing that like a good man I always supported the right and made justice, as I should, the first thing? No indeed, men of Athens, neither I nor any other. I have been always the same in all my actions, public as well as private, and never have yielded to any base agreement with those who are slanderously termed my disciples, or to any other. The truth is I have no regular disciples, but if anyone likes to come and hear me while I am pursuing my mission, whether he be young or old, he may freely come. Nor do I converse with those who pay only, and not with those who do not pay; but anyone, whether he be rich or poor, may question and answer me and listen to my words. If he turns out to be a bad man or a good one, I am not responsible, as I never taught him anything. If anyone says he has ever learned or heard anything from me in private which all the world has not heard, I would like you to know that he is lying.

Underline the major point Socrates makes in this paragraph.

I will be asked, why do people delight in continually conversing with you? I have told you already, Athenians, the whole truth about this. They like to hear the cross-examination of the pretenders to wisdom; there is amusement in this. This is a duty which the gods have imposed upon me, as I am assured by oracles, visions, and in every sort of way which the will of divine power was ever made plain to anyone. This is true, O Athenians or, if not true, would be soon refuted. If I am really corrupting the youth and have corrupted some of them already, those who have grown up and are aware I gave them bad advice in the days of their youth should come forward as accusers and take their revenge. If they do not like to come themselves, some of their relatives, fathers, brothers, or other kinsmen should say what evil their families suffered at my hands. Now is their time. I see many of them in the court.

There is Crito, who is of the same age and of the same township as myself, and there is Critobulus, his son, whom I also see. There is Lysanias of Sphettus, who is the father of Aeschines—he is present; and also there is Antiphon of Cephisus, who is the father of Epigenes; and there are the brothers of several who have associated with me. There is Nicostratus the son of Theosdotides, and the brother of Theodotus (not Theodotus himself—he is dead, and therefore, he will not seek to stop him). There is Paralus, the son of Demodocus, who had a brother Theages; and Adeimantus, the son of Ariston, whose brother Plato is present; and Aeantodorus, who is the brother of Apollodorus, whom I also see. I might mention a great many others, any of whom Meletus could have produced as witnesses in the course of his speech. Let him still produce them, if he has forgotten—I will make way for him. Let him speak, if he has any testimony of this sort which he can produce. Nay, Athenians, the very opposite is the truth. For all these are ready to witness on behalf of the corruptor, of the destroyer of their kindred, as Meletus and Anytus call me; not the corrupted youth only—there might have been a motive for that—but their uncorrupted elder relatives. Why should they too support me with their testimony? Why indeed, except for the reason of truth and justice, and because they know I am speaking the truth and Meletus is lying.

Well, Athenians, this and similar to this is nearly all the defense I have to offer. Yet a word more. Perhaps there may be someone who is offended by me, when he calls to mind how he himself on a similar, or even a less serious occasion, had recourse to prayers and supplications with many tears, and how he produced his children in court, which was a moving spectacle, together with a group of his relations and friends. I, who am probably in danger of my life, will do none of these things. Perhaps this may come into his mind and he may be set against me and vote in anger because he is displeased at this. Now if there is such a person among you I reply to him: My friend, I am a man, and like other men, a creature of flesh and blood and not of wood or stone, as Homer says.[9] I have a family, yes, and sons, O Athenians, three in number, one of whom is growing up and two others who are still young. Yet I will not bring any of them here in order to beg you for an acquittal. And why not? Not from any self-will or disregard of you. Whether I am, or am not, afraid of death is another question, of which I will not now speak. My reason is that I feel such conduct to be discreditable to myself, you, and the whole state. One who has reached my years and who has a name for wisdom, whether deserved or not, should not lower himself. The world has decided that Socrates is in some way superior to other men. And if those among you who are said to be superior in wisdom, courage, and any other virtue lower themselves in this way, how shameful is their conduct!

I have seen men of reputation, when they have been condemned, behaving in the strangest manner. They seemed to believe they were going to suffer something dreadful if they died, and they could be immortal if you only allowed them to live. I think they were a dishonor to the state, and any stranger coming in would say the most eminent men of Athens, to whom the Athenians themselves give honor and command, are no better than women. I say these things ought not to be done by those of us who are of reputation; and if they are done, you ought not to permit them. You ought to show you are more inclined to condemn, not the man who is quiet, but the man who gets up a doleful scene and makes the city ridiculous.

Setting aside the question of dishonor, there seems to be something wrong in begging a judge and thus procuring an acquittal instead of informing and convincing him. For his duty is not to make a present of justice, but to give judgment. He has sworn he will judge according to the laws and not according to his own

Stop again and think about what you read. The major points

established since page 44 were: ___

_____

_____

_____

_____

_____

_____

_____

_____

The number of lines you drew

across the page is _____ .
Continue to divide the *Apology* into logical units and underline important points. Practice adding your own notes in the margin.

good pleasure. Neither he nor we should get into the habit of perjuring ourselves—there can be no piety in that. Do not require me to do what I consider dishonorable, impious, and wrong, especially now, when I am being tried for impiety on the indictment of Meletus. For if, O men of Athens, by force of persuasion and entreaty, I could overpower your oaths, then I should be teaching you to believe there are no gods and convict myself in my own defense of not believing in them. But that is not the case. I do believe there are gods and in a far higher sense than any of my accusers believe in them. To you and to the gods I commit my cause, to be determined by you as is best for you and me.

(The jury returns a guilty verdict and Meletus proposes death as punishment.)

There are many reasons why I am not grieved, O men of Athens, at the vote of condemnation. I expected this and am only surprised the votes are so nearly equal. I thought the majority against me would have been far larger, but now, had thirty votes gone over to the other side, I would have been acquitted. And I may say I have escaped Meletus' charges. And I may say more; without the assistance of Anytus and Lycon, he would not have had a fifth part of the votes, as the law requires, in which case he would have incurred a fine of a thousand drachmae.

He proposes death as the penalty. What shall I propose on my part, O men of Athens? Clearly what is my due. What is that which I ought to pay or to receive? What shall be done to the man who has never been idle during his whole life, but has been careless of what the many care about—wealth, family interests, military offices and speaking in the Assembly, and courts, plots, and parties. Believing I was really too honest a man to follow in this way and live, I did not go where I could do no good to you or to myself. I went where I could do the greatest good privately to every one of you. I sought to persuade every man among you that he must look to himself and seek virtue and wisdom before he looks to his private interests, and look to the welfare of the State before he looks to the wealth of the State. This should be the order which he observes in all his actions. What shall be done to someone like me? Doubtless some good thing, O men of Athens, if he has his reward and the good should be suitable to him. What would be a reward suitable to a poor man who is your benefactor, who desires to instruct you? There can be no more fitting reward than maintenance in the Prytaneum,[10] O men of Athens, a reward which he deserves far more than the citizen who wins the prize at Olympia in the horse or chariot race, whether the chariots were drawn by two horses or many. For I am in need and he has

Group of elders that sat around all day

enough. He only gives you the appearance of happiness and I give you the reality. Thus, if I am to estimate the penalty justly, I say maintenance in the Prytaneum is just.

Perhaps you think I am mocking you in saying this, as in what I said before about the tears and prayers. But that is not the case. I speak because I am convinced I never intentionally wronged anyone, although I cannot convince you of that—for we have had a short conversation only. If there were a law at Athens, such as there is in other cities, that a case involving the death penalty should not be decided in one day, then I believe I would have convinced you. Now the time is too short. I cannot quickly refute great slanders and, as I am convinced that I never wronged another, I will assuredly not wrong myself. I will not say of myself that I deserve any evil, nor propose any penalty. Why should I? Because I am afraid of the penalty of death which Meletus proposes? When I do not know whether death is a good or an evil, why should I propose a penalty which would certainly be an evil? Shall I say imprisonment? And why should I live in prison, and be the slave of the judges of the year—of the Eleven? Or shall the penalty be a fine, and imprisonment until the fine is paid? There is the same objection. I should have to stay in prison for I have no money and cannot pay. And if I say exile, and this may be the penalty which you will affix, I must indeed be blinded by love of life, if I do not realize that if you, who are my own citizens, cannot endure my words and have found them so hateful you want to silence them, others are not likely to endure me. No indeed, men of Athens, that is not very likely. And what a life should I lead, at my age, wandering from city to city, living in ever-changing exile and always being driven out! For I am quite sure that whatever place I go, the young men will come to me. If I drive them away, their elders will drive me out. And, if I let them come, their fathers and friends will drive me out for their sakes.

Someone will say: Yes, Socrates, but can you not hold your tongue and then go into a foreign city, and no one will interfere with you? Now I have great difficulty in making you understand my answer to this. If I tell you this would be a disobedience to a divine command, and therefore I cannot hold my tongue, you will not believe I am serious. If I say again that greatest good is daily to converse about virtue and all that concerning which you hear me examining myself and others, and that the life which is unexamined is not worth living—that you are still less likely to believe. And yet what I say is true, although it is hard for me to persuade you. Moreover, I am not accustomed to thinking I deserve any punishment. Had I money I might have proposed to give you what I had and would have been none the worse. But you see I

Socrates' point in the "penalty" he proposes seems to be _____

_____

_____

_____ .

Number the alternative penalties Socrates rejects.

Vote: Guilty

Verdict: Death

have none and can only ask you to proportion the fine to my means. However, I think I could afford a mina, and therefore I propose that penalty. Plato, Crito, Critobulus, and Apollodorus, my friends here, bid me say 30 minae and they will pay the fine. Well, then, say 30 minae, let that be the penalty for that they will be ample security to you.

(The jury votes again to decide between Socrates' proposal of a fine and Meletus' proposal of the death penalty. The verdict is death.)

Not much time will be gained, O Athenians, in return for the evil name you will get from the enemies of the city, who will say you killed Socrates, a wise man. They will call me wise even though I am not wise when they want to reproach you. If you waited a little while, your desire would have been fulfilled in the course of nature. I am far advanced in years, as you may perceive, and not far from death. I am speaking now only to those of you who have condemned me to death. And I have another thing to say to them: You think I was convicted through deficiency of words—I mean, if I had thought fit to leave nothing undone, nothing unsaid, I might have gained an acquittal. Not so, the deficiency which led to my conviction was not of words—certainly not. I did not have the boldness or impudence or inclination to address you as you would have liked me to address you, weeping, wailing, and lamenting, and saying and doing many things which you have been accustomed to hear from others, and which, as I say, are unworthy of me. I believed I should not do anything common or cowardly in the hour of danger. I do not now repent the manner of my defense. I would rather die having spoken after my manner than speak in your manner and live. Neither in war nor yet at law ought any man to use every way of escaping death. Often in battle there is no doubt if a man will throw away his arms and fall on his knees before his pursuers, he may escape death. In other dangers there are other ways of escaping death, if a man is willing to say and do anything.

The difficulty, my friends, is not in avoiding death, but in avoiding evil; for evil runs faster than death. I am old and move slowly, and the slower runner has overtaken me, and my accusers are keen and quick, and the faster runner, who is evil, has overtaken them. And now I depart hence condemned by you to suffer the penalty of death, and they too go their ways condemned by the truth to suffer the penalty of wickedness. I must abide by my award—let them abide by theirs. I suppose these things may be regarded as fated—and I think things are as they should be.

And now, O men who have condemned me, I would prophesy to you. I am about to die and that is the hour in which men are

Socrates' mood is _____
_____
_____
because _____
_____
_____
_____ .

Note the comparison Socrates makes here.

gifted with prophetic power. I prophesy to you who are my murderers that, immediately after my death, punishment far heavier than you have inflicted on me will await you. You have killed me because you wanted to escape the accuser, and not to give an account of your lives. That will not be as you suppose. I say there will be more accusers of you than there are now, accusers I have restrained: And as they are younger they will be more severe with you and you will be more offended at them. For if you think that by killing men you can avoid the accuser censuring your lives, you are mistaken; that is not a way of escape which is either possible or honorable. The easiest, noblest way is not to be crushing others but to be improving yourselves. This is the prophecy which I utter before my departure to the members of the jury who have condemned me.

Socrates' prophecy is that _____ _____ _____ _____ _____ _____ _____ .

Friends who have acquitted me, I would like also to talk with you about this thing which has happened, while the judges are busy, and before I go to the place where I must die. Stay awhile, for we may as well talk with one another while there is time. You are my friends and I would like to show you the meaning of this event which has happened to me. O my judges—for you I may truly call judges—I should like to tell you of a wonderful occurrence. Before this, the spiritual voice within me has constantly been in the habit of opposing me even about trifles, if I was going to make a slip or error about anything. Now, as you see there has come upon me what may be thought, and is generally believed to be, the last and worst evil. But the spiritual voice made no sign of opposition, either as I was leaving my house and going out in the morning, or when I was going up into this court, or while I was speaking at anything I was going to say. I have often been stopped in the middle of a speech, but now in nothing I either said or did has the spiritual voice opposed me. Why is this? I will tell you. I regard this as a proof that what has happened to me is a good, and that those of us who think that death is an evil are in error. This is a great proof to me of what I am saying, for the customary sign would surely have opposed me had I been going to evil and not to good.

Let us reflect in another way, and we shall see there is great reason to hope that death is a good. Either death is a state of nothingness and utter unconsciousness, or, as men say, there is a change and migration of the soul from this world to another. Now if you suppose there is no consciousness, but a sleep like the sleep of him who is undisturbed even by the sight of dreams, death will be an unspeakable gain. If a person were to select the night in which his sleep was undisturbed even by dreams and were to compare this with the other days and nights of his life, and then were to tell us how many days and nights he passed in the course

Socrates believes that death might be a good because _____ _____ _____ _____ _____ _____ .

Socrates' points about death are

_____
_____
_____
_____
_____
_____.

Socrates might be happy to die

"again and again" because _____

_____
_____
_____
_____
_____.

of his life better and more pleasantly than this one, I think any man, even a great king, will not find many such days or nights, when compared with the others. Now if death is like this, I say to die is to gain, for eternity is then only a single night. But if death is the journey to another place, and there, as men say, all the dead are, what good, O my friends and judges, can be greater than this? If indeed when the traveler arrives in the other world, he is delivered from the false judges in this world and finds the true judges who are said to give judgment there, Minos, Rhadamanthus, Aeacus, and Triptolemus,[11] and other sons of the gods who were righteous in their own life, that journey will be worth making. What would a man give if he might converse with Orpheus and Masaeus and Hesiod and Homer?[12] Nay, if this is true, let me die again and again. I, too, shall have a wonderful interest in a place where I can converse with Palamedes, and Ajax, the son of Telamon,[13] and other heroes of old who have suffered death through an unjust judgment. I think there will be pleasure in comparing my own sufferings with theirs. Above all, I shall be able to continue my search into true and false knowledge. As in this world, so also in that; I shall find out who is wise and who pretends to be wise but is not. What would a man give, O judges, to be able to examine the leader of the great Trojan expedition, or Odysseus or Sisyphus,[14] or numberless others, men and women too! What infinite delight would there be in conversing with them and asking them questions! For in that world they do not put a man to death for such investigations, certainly not. For besides being happier in that world than in this, they will be immortal, if what is said is true.

Wherefore, O judges, be of good cheer about death, and know this truth—no evil can happen to a good man, either in life or after death. He and his are not neglected by the gods nor has my own approaching end happened by mere chance. I see clearly that to die and be released was better for me and therefore my spiritual voice gave no sign. Because of this also, I am not angry with my accusers or my condemners. They have done me no harm, although neither of them meant to do me any good; and for this I gently blame them.

Still I have a favor to ask of them. When my sons are grown up, I would ask you, O my friends, to punish them. I would have you trouble them, as I troubled you, if they seem to care about riches, or anything, more than virtue. Or, if they pretend to be something when they are really nothing, then chastise them, as I chastised you, for not caring about what they ought to care, and thinking they are something when they are really nothing. And if you do this, I and my sons will have received justice at your hands.

The hour of departure has arrived, and we go on our different ways—I to die, and you to live. Which is better only the god knows.

Thinking about the Apology

1. The *Apology* is the best source on our tour for discovering Plato's view of his teacher, Socrates. What did you learn about Socrates' life?

A great deal. He believes he has two groups of accusers. The first group is _____

_____

_____ and the second is _____

___ _____

_____. He tells a story about the oracle of Delphi partly to explain his bad reputation. The main points in the story are ___ _____

_____

_____

_____

_____

_____. Other things I learned about Socrates' life were _____

_____

_____

_____

_____ .

2. Now, think about Socrates' conversation with Meletus. Why does Socrates mention horse trainers?

This is an important part of his refutation of Meletus. Looking back at the dialogue, I see the point he makes specifically about horses and horse trainers is _____

_____

_____

_____ . The way this applies to Meletus is that ___ _____

_____

_____

_____

_____. Socrates is trying to show

the members of the jury that Meletus is _____

_____

_____

_____

_____

_____.

3. Shortly after this, Socrates says to Meletus, "you have just admitted that the good do their neighbors good, and the evil do them evil. Now, is that a truth which your superior wisdom has recognized thus early in life, and am I, at my age, in such a darkness and ignorance as not to know if a man with whom I have to associate is corrupted by me, I am very likely to be harmed by him? Yet you say I corrupt him and intentionally, too; of that you will never persuade me or any other human being. But either I do not corrupt them, or I corrupt them unintentionally, so that on either view of the case you lie. If my offense is unintentional, the laws do not mention unintentional offenses. You ought to have taken me aside and warned me, because if I had been better advised, I should have stopped doing what I only did unintentionally—no doubt I should."

What points does Socrates make here?

Socrates makes several interesting points. He says he either corrupts the youth intentionally or unintentionally. The reason

he says he could not be corrupting them intentionally is _____

_____

_____

_____

_____. And if he has been

corrupting them unintentionally, then _____

_____

_____

_____

_____. In either case

bringing Socrates to court is wrong. It is wrong in the first

case because _____

_____

_____

_____

_____. And it is obviously wrong in the

second case because _____

_____

_____

_____ .

4. At one point Socrates compares himself to a gadfly (a horsefly)
and Athens to a "great and noble steed." Why?

   Socrates believes he is like a gadfly because _____

_____

_____. Perhaps an example of

this from the *Euthyphro* is _____

_____

_____ .

5. Still later Socrates says, "I say again the greatest good of
man is daily to converse about virtue and all that concerning
which you hear me examining myself and others, and that the
life which is unexamined is not worth living. . . ."

   The pre-Socratic philosophers like Thales were all interested
in one thing. Contrast their interest with Socrates' in this statement.

   As you saw earlier in the tour, the pre-Socratics were all

trying to answer the same question. That question was _____

_____

_____

_____. A major change, occurring with

Socrates, as illustrated by this quotation, is _____

_____

_____

_____

_____. The relationship between this

concern and his story about the oracle at Delphi is _____

_____

_____

_____

_____ .

6. One thing Plato attempts in this dialogue is to draw a large
contrast between Socrates and the majority of the people in
Athens. How would you sum up the difference between them?

    Socrates is _____

_____

_____

_____

_____. The people of Athens would _____

_____

_____

_____

_____

_____ .

7. Now it is time for your verdict. Weigh your judgment carefully, but to simplify matters, perhaps you should stick to the
single charge of "corrupting the youth."

    From Meletus' point of view, Socrates is guilty of corrupting

the youth because _____

_____

_____

_____

_____

_____. Meletus would probably define

corruption as _____

_____

_____

_____

_____. According to Meletus, someone
who did not corrupt the youth but taught them correctly would
be someone who ___ _____

_____

_____

_____

_____. From Socrates' point of view,
he is not a corruptor of the youth because _____

_____

_____

_____

_____. Someone who would truly corrupt the
youth from his point of view would be _____

_____

_____

_____. In Socrates' opinion the best education
youth could have would involve _____

_____

_____

_____

_____. Choosing between Meletus and
Socrates, I would say _____

_____

_____

_____

_____

_____

_____

_____. An example of the truth of

my view is _____

_____

_____. In conclusion, _____

_____

_____

_____

_____

_____.

    Thinking back on the tour thus far, the five most important things I've learned are:

a. _____

_____

b. _____

_____

c. _____

_____

d. _____

_____

e. _____

_____

Apology *Quiz*

In order to get an overview of the general structure of the *Apology*, arrange the following in the order, 1–8, that they occur in the dialogue: Socrates' service as a soldier, the story about the oracle at Delphi, Socrates proposes his punishment, the refutation of the older accusers, the refutation of the newer accusers, Socrates confronts Meletus, the death verdict, the guilty verdict, Socrates tells about resisting the Thirty.

1.

2.

3.

4.

5.

6.

7.

8.

9. At the time of his trial, Socrates was_____ years old.

10. According to Socrates, he is charged with: (direct quote).

"_____

_____

_____

_____."

Socrates is famous for irony, that is, saying one thing and meaning another. Decide if the following are Ironic (I) or Non-ironic (N).

11. I or N: Socrates claims that the "persuasive words" of his accusers "almost made me forget who I was, such was their effect."

12. I or N: " . . . this is the first time I've appeared in a court of law."

13. I or N: "I have had many accusers who accused me in the past and their false charges have continued during many years."

14. I or N: Socrates claims he has no wisdom and is only wise in knowing that he is not wise.

15. I or N: Socrates says he questioned others in order to support the view of the oracle at Delphi that he is the wisest of mortals. "And so I go my way, obedient to the gods, and seek wisdom of anyone, whether citizen or stranger who appears to be wise. If he is not wise, then in support of the oracle I show him he is not wise."

16. I or N: After being condemned to death, Socrates says, "I am about to die and that is the hour in which men are gifted with prophetic power. I prophesy to you who are my murderers that, immediately after my death, punishment far heavier than you have inflicted on me will await you."

Near the end of the *Apology,* Socrates says, "The difficulty, my friends, is not in avoiding death, but in avoiding evil; for evil runs faster than death. I am old and move slowly, and the slower runner has overtaken me, and my accusers are keen and quick, and the faster runner, who is evil, has overtaken them."

17. The slower runner who has overtaken Socrates is _____ .

18. The four participants in the "race" are: _____
_____ .

19. T or F: Socrates points out the paradox that even though he is slower, he has beaten his fast accusers by arriving at death before they have.

20. T or F: Socrates points out the paradox that even though he is slow, he has not been overtaken yet by death, the fast runner who overtakes everyone.

21. T or F: Socrates points out the paradox that even though he is old and slow he has not been overtaken by evil, which is fast.

22. T or F: Socrates sees evil as fast because it is more likely to catch an individual before death.

Vote and Debate

1. Socrates was guilty of believing in new gods.

Agree ____ Disagree ____ Evidence: _____
_____
_____
_____ .

2. Socrates was guilty of making the weaker argument defeat the stronger.

Agree ____ Disagree ____ Evidence: _____
_____
_____
_____ .

3. Socrates wanted to die and thus did not defend himself as strongly as he might have.

Agree ____ Disagree ____ Evidence: _____ _____

_____

_____

_____.

/3/ CRITO

Preview

The *Crito* takes place in the jail where Socrates awaits execution. The dialogue is a debate between Socrates and Crito, his old friend, about whether Socrates should escape.

Annotation Tasks

Background Information. In the first few pages, underline the time of day, the personality differences between Socrates and Crito, and Socrates' prophetic dream.

Main Theme. In the remaining dialogue look for Crito's reasons in favor of Socrates' escape and the main points in Socrates' argument in favor of remaining in jail.

Crito

SOCRATES: Why have you come at this hour, Crito? It must be quite early?

CRITO: Yes, it certainly is.

SOC: What time is it?

CR: The dawn is breaking.

SOC: I am surprised the keeper of the prison let you in.

CR: He knows me because I come often, Socrates, and he owes me a favor.

SOC: Did you just get here?

CR: No, I came some time ago.

SOC: Then why did you sit and say nothing, instead of waking me at once?

CR: Why, indeed, Socrates, I myself would rather not have all this sleeplessness and sorrow. I have been wondering at your peaceful slumber and that was the reason why I did not [wake] you. I wanted you to be out of pain. I always thought you fortunate in your calm temperament but I never saw anything like the easy, cheerful way you bear this calamity.

SOC: Crito, when a man reaches my age he should not fear approaching death.

CR: Other men of your age in similar situations fear death.

SOC: That may be. But you have not told me why you come at this early hour.

CR: I bring you a sad and painful message; not sad, as I believe, for you, but to all of us who are your friends, and saddest of all to me.

SOC: Has the ship come from Delos, on the arrival of which I am to die?

CR: No, the ship has not actually arrived, but it will probably be here today because people who came from Sunium tell me they left it there. Therefore, tomorrow, Socrates, will be the last day of your life.

SOC: Very well, Crito. If it is the will of the gods, I am willing, but I believe there will be a delay of a day.

CR: Why do you say that?

SOC: I will tell you. I am to die on the day after the arrival of the ship?

CR: Yes, that is what the authorities say.

SOC: I do not think the ship will be here until tomorrow. I had a dream last night, or rather only just now, when you fortunately allowed me to sleep.

CR: What was your dream?

SOC: I saw the image of a wondrously beautiful woman, clothed in white robes, who called to me and said: "O Socrates, the third day hence to fertile Phthia shalt thou go."[1]

CR: What a strange dream, Socrates!

SOC: I think there can be no doubt about the meaning, Crito.

CR: Perhaps the meaning is clear to you. But, oh my beloved Socrates, let me beg you once more to take my advice and escape! If you die I shall not only lose a friend who can never be replaced, but there is also another evil: People who do not know you and me will believe I might have saved you if I had been willing to spend money, but I did not care to do so. Now, can there be a worse disgrace than this—that I should be thought to value money more than the life of a friend? The many will not be persuaded I wanted you to escape and you refused.

A major difference already established between Socrates and Crito is _____ _____ _____ _____ .

In general, the relationship between the two men is _____ _____ _____ _____ .

Here and on the next two pages, number each reason Crito gives Socrates to escape. There are at least eight.

65

SOC: But why, my dear Crito, should we care about the opinion of the many? Good men, and they are the only persons worth considering, will think of these things as they happened.

CR: But do you see, Socrates, the opinion of the many must be regarded, as is clear in your own case, because they can do the very greatest evil to anyone who has lost their good opinion.

SOC: I only wish, Crito, they could. Then they could also do the greatest good and that would be excellent. The truth is, they can do neither good nor evil. They cannot make a man wise or make him foolish, and whatever they do is the result of chance.

CR: Well, I will not argue about that. But please tell me, Socrates, if you are acting out of concern for me and your other friends. Are you afraid if you escape we may get into trouble with the informers for having stolen you away and lose either the whole or a great part of our property, or an even worse evil may happen to us? Now, if this is your fear, be at ease. In order to save you we should surely run this, or even a greater, risk. Be persuaded, then, and do as I say.

SOC: Yes, Crito, that is one fear which you mention, but by no means the only one.

CR: Do not be afraid. There are persons who at no great cost are willing to save you and bring you out of prison. As for the informers, they are reasonable in their demands, a little money will satisfy them. My resources, which are ample, are at your service and if you are troubled about spending all mine, there are strangers who will give you theirs. One of them, Simmias the Theban, brought a sum of money for this very purpose. Cebes and many others are willing to spend their money, too. I say, therefore, do not hesitate about making your escape and do not say, as you did in the court, you will have difficulty in knowing what to do with yourself if you escape. Men will love you in other places you may go and not only in Athens. There are friends of mine in Thessaly, if you wish to go to them, who will value and protect you; and no Thessalian will give you any trouble. Nor can I think you are justified, Socrates, in betraying you own life when you might be saved. This is playing into the hands of your enemies and destroyers. Besides, I say you are betraying your children. You should bring them up and educate them; instead you go away and leave them, and they will have to grow up on their own. If they do not meet with the usual fate of orphans, there will be small thanks to you. No man should bring children into the world who is unwilling to continue their nurture and education. You are choosing the easier part, as I think, not the better and manlier, which you should as one who professes virtue in all his actions. Indeed, I am ashamed not only of you, but also of us, your friends, when I think this entire business of yours will be attributed to our lack of courage. The trial need never have started or might have been brought to another conclusion. The end of it all, which is the crowning absurdity, will seem to have been permitted by us, through cowardice and baseness, who might have saved you. You might have saved yourself, if we had been good for anything, for there was no difficulty in escaping, and we did not see how disgraceful, Socrates, and also miserable all this will be to us as well as to you. Make up your mind then. Or rather, have your mind already made up, for the time of deliberation is over. There is only one thing to be done, which must be done if at all this very night, and which any delay will render all but impossible. I plead with you therefore, Socrates, to be persuaded by me, and do as I say.

SOC: Dear Crito, your zeal is invaluable if right. If wrong, the greater the zeal the greater the evil. Therefore, we must consider whether these things should be done or not. I am, and always have been, someone who must be guided by reason, whatever the reason may be which, upon reflection, appears to me to be the best. Now that this misfortune has come upon me, I cannot put away my old beliefs. The principles I honored and revered I still honor; and unless we can find other and better principles, I will not agree with you. I would not even if the power of the multitude could inflict many more imprisonments, confiscations, and deaths, frightening us like children with foolish terrors.

Now, go back and put a star by the best reasons, according to you, for escaping.

What will be the best way of considering the question? Shall I return to your old argument about the opinions of men, some of which should be considered, and others, as we were saying, are not to be considered. Now were we right in maintaining this before I was condemned? And has the argument, which was once good, now proved to be talk for the sake of talking—in fact an amusement only and altogether foolish? That is what I want to consider with your help, Crito: whether, under my present circumstances, the argument appears to be in any way different or not and is to be followed by me or abandoned. That argument, I believe, held by many who claim to be authorities, was to the effect that the opinions of some men are to be considered and of other men not to be considered. Now you, Crito, are not going to die tomorrow—at least, there is no probability of this. You are therefore not likely to be deceived by the circumstances in which you are placed. Tell me, then, whether I am right in saying that some opinions are to be valued and other opinions are not to be valued. I ask you whether I was right in believing this?

On the following pages, underline each of the main points in Socrates' answer to Crito.

CR: Certainly.

SOC: The good opinions are to be believed and not the bad?

CR: Yes.

SOC: And the opinions of the wise are good and the opinions of the foolish are evil?

CR: Certainly.

SOC: And what was said about another matter? Is the gymnastics student supposed to attend to the praise and blame and opinion of every man, or of one man only—his physician or trainer, whoever that is?

CR: Of one man only.

SOC: And he should fear the blame and welcome praise of that one only, and not of the many?

CR: That is clear.

SOC: He should live and train, eat and drink in the way which seems good to his single teacher who has understanding, rather than according to the opinion of all other men put together?

CR: True.

SOC: And if he disobeys and rejects the opinion and approval of the one, and accepts the opinion of the many who have no understanding, will he not suffer evil?

CR: Certainly he will.

SOC: And how will the evil affect the disobedient student?

CR: Clearly, it will affect his body; that is what is destroyed by the evil.

SOC: Very good. Is this not true, Crito, of other things which we need not separately consider? In the matter of the just and unjust, the fair and foul, the good and evil, which are the subjects of our present discussion, should we follow the opinion of the many and fear them, or the opinion of the one man who has understanding? Is he the one we ought to fear and honor more than all the rest of the world? If we leave him, we shall destroy and injure that principle in us which may be assumed to be improved by justice and deteriorated by injustice? Is there not such a principle?

CR: Certainly there is, Socrates.

SOC: Take a similar case. If, acting under the advice of men who have no understanding, we ruined what is improved by health and destroyed by disease—would life be worth having? You understand I mean the body?

CR: Yes.

SOC: Could we live having an evil and corrupted body?

CR: Certainly not.

SOC: And will life be worth having, if the soul is crippled, which is improved by justice and harmed by injustice? Do we suppose the soul to be inferior to the body?

CR: Certainly not.

SOC: More important, then?

CR: Far more important.

SOC: Then, my friend, we must not consider what the many say of us, but what he, the one man who has understanding of the just and unjust will say, and what the truth will say. Therefore you begin in error when you suggest we should consider the opinion of the many about the just and unjust, the good and evil, the honorable and dishonorable, but what if someone says, "But the many can kill us."

CR: Yes, Socrates, that will clearly be the answer.

SOC: Still I believe our old argument is unshaken. I would like to know whether I may say the same of another proposition—that not life, but a good life, is to be chiefly valued?

CR: Yes, that is also true.

SOC: And a good life is equivalent to a just and honorable one—that is also true?

CR: Yes, that is true.

SOC: From these beliefs I am ready to consider whether I should or should not try to escape without the consent of the Athenians. If I am clearly right in escaping, then I will make the attempt, but if not, I will remain here. The other considerations which you mention, of money and loss of reputation and the duty of educating children, are, I fear, only the beliefs of the many, who would be as ready to bring people to life, if they were able, as they are to put them to death. The only question remaining to be considered is whether we shall do right escaping or allowing others to aid our escape and paying them money and thanks or whether we shall not do right. If the latter, then neither death nor any other calamity which may result from my remaining here must be allowed to influence us.

CR: I think you are right, Socrates. But, how shall we proceed?

SOC: Let us consider the matter together and either refute me if you can and I will be convinced; or else cease, my dear friend, from repeating to me that I ought to escape against the wishes of the Athenians. I am extremely eager to be persuaded by you, but not against my own better judgment. And now please consider my first position and do your best to answer me.

CR: I will do my best.

SOC: Are we to say we are never intentionally to do wrong, or that in one way we should and in another way we should not do wrong? Or is doing wrong always evil and dishonorable, as I was just now saying? Are all our former admissions to be thrown away because of these last few days? Have we, at our age, been earnestly discoursing with one another all our life long only to discover we are no better than children? Or, are we convinced in spite of the opinion of the many and in spite of consequences of the truth of what we said, that injustice is always an evil and dishonor to him who acts unjustly? Shall we agree to that?

CR: Yes.

SOC: Then we must do no wrong?

CR: Certainly not.

Crito has been wrong because _____ _____ _____ _____ _____ _____ .

Several of Crito's arguments are dismissed here because _____ _____ _____ _____ .

SOC: Nor when injured should we injure in return, as the many imagine. We must injure no one at all?

CR: Clearly not.

SOC: Again, Crito, can we do evil?

CR: Surely not, Socrates.

SOC: And what of doing evil in return for evil, which is the morality of the many—is that just or not?

CR: Not just.

SOC: For doing evil to another is the same as injuring him.

CR: Very true.

A similar Christian belief is _____ _____ _____ _____ _____ .

SOC: Then we ought not to retaliate or render evil for evil to any one, whatever evil we may have suffered from him. But I would have you consider, Crito, whether you really mean what you are saying. For this opinion has never been held, and never will be held, by many people. Those who are agreed and those who are not agreed upon this point have no common ground, and can only despise one another when they see how widely they differ. Tell me, then, whether you agree with my first principle, that neither injury nor retaliation nor returning evil for evil is ever right. Shall that be the premise of our argument? Or do you disagree? For this has been and still is my opinion; but, if you are of another opinion, let me hear what you have to say. If, however, you remain of the same mind as formerly, I will go to the next step.

CR: You may proceed, for I have not changed my mind.

SOC: The next step may be put in the form of a question: Ought a man to do what he admits to be right, or ought he to betray the right?

CR: He ought to do what he thinks right.

SOC: But if this is true, what is the application? In leaving the prison against the will of the Athenians, do I wrong anyone? Or do I wrong those whom I ought least to wrong? Do I abandon the principles which were acknowledged by us to be just? What do you say?

CR: I cannot tell, Socrates, because I do not know.

At this point, Socrates ends his review of his past beliefs and begins a long, internal dialogue. The major points established thus

far are: _____

_____

_____

_____

_____

_____

_____ .

SOC: Then consider the matter in this way—imagine I am about to escape, and the Laws and the State come and interrogate me: "Tell us, Socrates," they say, "what are you doing? Are you going to overturn us—the Laws and the State, as far as you are able? Do you imagine that a State can continue and not be overthrown, in which the decisions of Law have no power, but are set aside and overthrown by individuals?"

What will be our answer, Crito, to these and similar words? Anyone, and especially a clever orator, will have a good deal to say about the evil of setting aside the Law which requires a sentence to be carried out. We might reply, "Yes, but the State has injured us and given an unjust sentence." Suppose I say that?

CR: Very good, Socrates.

SOC: "And was that our agreement with you?" the Law would say, "Or were you to abide by the sentence of the State?" And if I were surprised at their saying this, the Law would probably add: "Answer, Socrates, instead of opening your eyes: you are in the habit of asking and answering questions. Tell us what complaint you have against us which justifies you in attempting to destroy us and the State? In the first place did we not bring you into existence? Your father married your mother by our aid and conceived you. Say whether you have any objection against those of us who regulate marriage?" None, I should reply. "Or against those of us who regulate the system of care and education of children in which you were trained? Were not the Laws, who have the charge of this, right in commanding your father to train you in the arts and exercise?" Yes, I should reply.

"Well then, since you were brought into the world, nurtured and educated by us, can you deny in the first place that you are our child and slave, as your fathers were before you? And if this is true you are not on equal terms with us. Nor can you think you have a right to do to us what we are doing to you. Would you have any right to strike or do any other evil to a father or to your master, if you had one, when you have been struck or received some other evil at his hands? And because we think it is right to destroy you, do you think that you have any right to destroy us in return, and your country so far as you are able? And will you, O expounder of virtue, say you are justified in this? Has a philosopher like you failed to discover your country is more to be valued and higher and holier by far than mother and father or any ancestor, and more regarded in the eyes of the gods and of men of understanding? It should be soothed and gently and reverently entreated when angry, even more than a father, and if not persuaded, it should be obeyed. And when we are punished by the State, whether with imprisonment or whipping, the punishment is to be endured in silence. If the State leads us to wounds or death in battle, we follow as is right; no one can yield or leave his rank, but whether in battle or in a court of law, or in any other place, he must do what his city and his country order him. Or, he must change their view of what is just. If he may do no violence to his father or mother, much less may he do violence to his country." What answer shall we make to this, Crito? Do the Laws speak truly, or do they not?

CR: I think that they do.

SOC: Then the Laws will say: "Consider, Socrates, if this is true, that in your present attempt you are going to do us wrong. For, after having brought you into the world, nurtured and educated you, and given you and every other citizen a share in every good

From this page until the end, number and underline each new reason Socrates gives Crito for not escaping.

The comparison Socrates makes is between _____

_____

and _____

_____ .

His point is _____

_____

_____

_____

_____

_____ .

Find and underline the sentence with three reasons for not escaping.

we had to give, we further give the right to every Athenian, if he does not like us when he has come of age and has seen the ways of the city, he may go wherever else he pleases and take his goods with him. None of us Laws will forbid or interfere with him. Any of you who does not like us and the city, and who wants to go to a colony or to any other city, may go where he likes, and take his possessions with him. But he who has experience of the way we order justice and administer the State, and still remains, has entered into an implied contract to do as we command him. He who disobeys us is, as we maintain, triply wrong; first, because in disobeying us he is disobeying his parents; second, because we are the authors of his education; third, because he has made an agreement with us that he will duly obey our commands. He neither obeys them nor convinces us our commands are wrong. We do not rudely impose our commands but give each person the alternative of obeying or convincing us. That is what we offer and he does neither. These are the sort of accusations to which, as we were saying, Socrates, you will be exposed if you do as you were intending; you, above all other Athenians."

Suppose I ask, why is this? They will justly answer that I above all other men have acknowledged the agreement.

"There is clear proof," they will say, "Socrates, that we and the city were not displeasing to you. Of all Athenians you have been the most constant resident in the city, which, as you never leave, you appear to love. You never went out of the city either to see the games, except once when you went to the Isthmus, or to any other place unless you were on military service; nor did you travel as other men do. Nor had you any curiosity to know other States or their Laws: Your affections did not go beyond us and our State; we were your special favorites and you agreed in our government of you. This is the State in which you conceived your children, which is a proof of your satisfaction. Moreover, you might, if you wished, have fixed the penalty at banishment in the course of the trial—the State which refuses to let you go now would have let you go then. You pretended you preferred death to exile and that you were not grieved at death. And now you have forgotten these fine sentiments and pay no respect to us, the Laws, whom you destroy. You are doing what only a miserable slave would do, running away and turning your back upon the agreements which you made as a citizen. First of all, answer this very question: Are we right in saying you agreed to be governed according to us in deed, and not in word only? Is that true or not?"

How shall we answer that, Crito? Must we not agree?

CR: We must, Socrates.

SOC: Then will the Laws say: "You, Socrates, are breaking the agreements which you made with us at your leisure, not in any haste or under any compulsion or deception, but having had 70 years to think of them, during which time you were at liberty to leave the city, if we were not to your liking or if our covenants appeared to you to be unfair. You might have gone either to Lacedaemon or Crete, which you often praise for their good government, or to some other Hellenic or foreign state. You, above all other Athenians, seemed to be so fond of the State and of us, her Laws, that you never left her. The lame, the blind, the maimed were not more stationary in the State than you were. Now you run away and forsake your agreements. Not, Socrates, if you will take our advice; do not make yourself ridiculous by escaping out of the city.

Continue underlining each new reason for not escaping.

"Just consider, if you do evil in this way, what good will you do either yourself or your friends? That your friends will be driven into exile and lose their citizenship, or will lose their property, is reasonably certain. You yourself, if you fly to one of the neighboring cities, like Thebes or Megara, both of which are well-governed cities, will come to them as an enemy, Socrates. Their government will be against you and all patriotic citizens will cast suspicious eye upon you as a destroyer of the Laws. You will confirm in the minds of the judges the justice of their own condemnation of you. For he who is a corruptor of the Laws is more than likely to be corruptor of the young. Will you then flee from well-ordered cities and virtuous men? Is existence worth having on these terms? Or will you go to these cities without shame and talk to them, Socrates? And what will you say to them? Will you say what you say here about virtue, justice, institutions, and laws being the best things among men. Would that be decent of you? Surely not.

"If you go away from well-governed states to Crito's friends in Thessaly, where there is a great disorder and immorality, they will be charmed to have the tale of your escape from prison, set off with ludicrous particulars of the manner in which you were wrapped in a goatskin or some other disguise and metamorphosed as the fashion of runaways is— that is very likely. But will there be no one to remind you in your old age you violated the most sacred laws from a miserable desire of a little more life? Perhaps not, if you keep them in a good temper. But if they are angry you will hear many degrading things; you will live, but how? As the flatterer of all men and the servant of all men. And doing what? Eating and drinking in Thessaly, having gone abroad in order that you may get a dinner. Where will your fine sentiments about justice and virtue be then? Say that you wish to live for the sake of your children, that you may bring them up and educate them—will you take them into Thessaly and deprive them of Athenian citizenship? Is that the benefit which you would confer upon them? Or are you under the impression that they will be better cared for and educated here if you are still alive, although absent from them because your friends will take care of them? Do you think if you are an inhabitant of Thessaly they will take care of them, and if you are an inhabitant of the other world they will not take care of them? No, if they who call themselves friends are truly friends, they surely will.

"Listen, then, Socrates, to us who have brought you up. Think not of life and children first, and of justice afterwards, but of justice first, that you may be justified before the rulers of the other world. For neither will you nor your children be happier or holier in this life, or happier in another, if you do as Crito bids. Now you depart in innocence, a sufferer and not a doer of evil; a victim, not of the Laws, but of men. But if you escape, returning evil for evil and injury for injury, breaking the agreements which you have made with us, and wronging those whom you ought least to wrong, that is to say, yourself, your friends, your country, and us, we shall be angry with you while you live. Our brethren, the Laws in the other world, will receive you as an enemy because they will know you have done your best to destroy us. Listen, then, to us and not to Crito."

This is the voice which I seem to hear murmuring in my ears, like the sound of a divine flute in the ears of the mystic. That voice, I say, is humming in my ears and prevents me from hearing any other. I know anything more which you may say will be useless. Yet speak, if you have anything to say.

CR: I have nothing to say, Socrates.

SOC: Then let me follow what seems to be the will of the god.

Socrates' most convincing arguments for not escaping were: _____
_____
_____
_____
_____
_____
_____
_____ .

Thinking about the Crito

1. Think of the *Crito* as falling into three large parts. The first part introduces the two main characters and states Crito's arguments for escaping. The second part reviews some of Socrates' past philosophical principles. The last part applies these principles to his present situation and presents arguments for not escaping.

Looking back at the notes in the margin, I see the first part ends on about page _____.

What we learn about the differences between Socrates and Crito is _____
_____
_____

_____. Crito's main arguments for

escaping are _____

_____

_____. What many of these arguments have

in common is _____

_____

_____

_____

_____. Thus, we see Crito is

a person who _____

_____

_____

_____. The principles Socrates'

states in the second part of the dialogue are his beliefs that ___

_____

_____

_____

_____. In the third section he

speaks to himself in the voice of the Laws. The points he makes

against escaping are _____

_____

_____

_____

_____.

2. Socrates asks, "When injured should we injure in return . . . ?"
To what two injuries does he refer?

The injury that has already occurred is _____

_____ . The other injury will be _____

_____

_____

_____ .

3. Assume you are Crito. Offer your best single argument to Socrates for escaping. Remember, you will not be successful if you try to get him to violate his principles.

I would say that there is at least one more argument in favor of your escape. I will state it briefly and then expand it.

In essence, my argument is _____

_____

_____

_____ . My reasons for saying this

are _____

_____

_____

_____ . What you have not realized is _____

_____

_____ . If you escape, you would not be

returning an injury for an injury because _____

_____

_____

_____ . Nor would you be harming

your soul as you fear because _____

_____

_____

_____

_____. Even though the
Laws are, in some sense, your guardians and parents, what you
should have replied to them is _____

_____

_____

_____

_____. I can even find
evidence for my view from your own life. When I look at
what you said in the *Apology* I see _____

_____

_____

_____

_____.

4. Now try your hand at composing a question on the *Crito.*

A good question to ask about the *Crito*, which would help a
careful reader see the dialogue more clearly, would be _____

_____

_____

_____

_____. And if you had asked me that fine
question, my answer would have been _____

_____

_____

_____

_____

_____.

Crito *Quiz*

Which of the following statements are consistent (C) or inconsistent (I) with Crito's reasons for Socrates to escape?

1. C or I: We should worry about what others think of us.

2. C or I: Living justly is more important than living.

3. C or I: Obey the will of the gods.

4. C or I: Athens is an unjust state.

5. C or I: By staying in jail, Socrates is contradicting his former ethical beliefs.

6. C or I: By staying in jail, Socrates is avoiding his responsibility as a parent.

7. C or I: Because he is old, Socrates should cling to his last few years.

8. C or I: Socrates' death will make his enemies happy.

9. C or I: Socrates has an obligation to his wife to escape.

10. C or I: There is no afterlife; therefore, Socrates should enjoy this life while he can.

11. C or I: Socrates conducted a weak defense at his trial.

Which of the following statements are consistent (C) or inconsistent (I) with Socrates' reasons for not escaping?

12. C or I: The Laws are like our parents.

13. C or I: The Laws are like gods.

14. C or I: We should keep our just agreements unless we violate the will of the gods in doing so.

15. C or I: It is not right to return a wrong for a wrong.

16. C or I: The soul and the body are of relatively equal value.

17. C or I: Immoral actions harm the soul.

18. C or I: Immoral actions will cause the gods to punish us.

19. C or I: Children should be free to look after their own education.

20. C or I: Socrates' friends will be punished if he escapes.

21. C or I: The members of the jury are wise; therefore, their verdict should be obeyed.

22. C or I: We should not listen to the opinions of the many.

23. C or I: The noblest death is dying for one's beliefs.

24. C or I: Choosing to spend one's life in a state constitutes an implicit agreement that the state's laws are just.

25. C or I: The gods punish cowardly actions.

Vote and Debate

1. Socrates should have taken Crito's offer and escaped from jail.

Agree —— Disagree —— Evidence: _____

_____

_____

_____.

2. Socrates did not believe in civil disobedience.

Agree —— Disagree —— Evidence: _____

_____

_____

_____.

3. Crito did not understand Socrates.

Agree —— Disagree —— Evidence: _____

_____

_____

_____.

4. Socrates did not understand Crito.

Agree —— Disagree —— Evidence: _____

_____

_____

_____.

/4/ THE DEATH SCENE FROM THE *PHAEDO*

399 BCE

Jacques-Louis David, *The Death of Socrates,* 1787. Read the following excerpt from the *Phaedo* and see if David's painting accurately reflects the character of Socrates and his friends.

Preview

The entire *Phaedo* is a long dialogue apparently written at about the middle of Plato's career. The dialogues you just traveled through on the tour are products of his early years as a philosopher. These first dialogues apply mainly to Socrates and his situation. The *Phaedo,* however, is not only a portrait of Socrates' last hours but also an ambitious attempt to describe the soul's relationship to the body and the soul's existence before birth and after death. After you read the following pages, which conclude the *Phaedo,* I hope you will want to read the entire work.

80

Background and Main Theme.　This brief selection describes the last moments of Socrates' life. Plato presents the story of Socrates' death as an account presented by Phaedo of Elis to Echecrates, an admirer of Socrates. The mood is so powerful I have not distracted you with anything in the margins. Underline the differences between Socrates and the witnesses of his death.

Phaedo *(the death scene)*

When he spoke these words, he arose and went into the bath chamber with Crito, who told us to wait. We waited, talking and thinking of the subject of discourse and also of the greatness of our sorrow. He was like a father we were losing, and we were about to spend the rest of our lives as orphans. When he had taken his bath, his children were brought to him; he had two young sons and an elder one; the women of his family also came, and he talked to them and gave them a few directions in the presence of Crito. He then dismissed them and returned to us.

Now the hour of sunset was near, for a long time had passed while he was within. When he came out he sat down with us again after his bath, but not much was said. Soon the jailer, who was the servant of the Eleven, entered and stood by him.

He said, "To you, Socrates, whom I know to be the noblest, gentlest, and best of all who ever came to this place, I know you do not have the angry feelings of other men who rage and swear at me, when, in obedience to the authorities, I ask them to drink the poison. Indeed, I am sure you will not be angry with me. Others, as you are aware, and not I, are the guilty cause. And so goodbye, and try to bear lightly what must be. You know my errand." Then bursting into tears, he turned away and went out.

Socrates looked at him and said, "I return your good wishes, and will do as you bid."

Then turning to us, he said, "How charming the man is. Since I have been in prison he always comes to see me, and at times he would talk to me and was as good as he could be to me. Now see how generously he sorrows for me. But we must do as he says, Crito. Let the cup be brought, if the poison is prepared. If not, let the attendant prepare some."

"But," said Crito, "the sun is still upon the hilltops and many have taken the draught late; and after the announcement has been made to him, he has eaten and drunk, and indulged in sensual delights. Do not hurry then; there is still time."

Socrates said, "Yes, Crito, and those you speak of are right in doing that, for they think they will gain by the delay. But, I am right in doing what I do because I do not think I would gain anything by drinking the poison a little later. I should be sparing a life which is already gone; I could only laugh at myself for this. Please then do as I say and do not refuse me."

Crito, when he heard this, made a sign to the servant. The servant went in, remained for some time and then returned with the jailer carrying the cup of poison.

Socrates said, "You, my good friend, who are experienced in these matters give me directions how I am to proceed."

The man answered, "You only have to walk about until your legs are heavy, then lie down, and the poison will act." At the same time he handed the cup to Socrates, who in the easiest and gentlest manner, without the least fear or change of color or feature, looking at the man with all his eyes, Echecrates, as his manner was, took the cup and said, "What do you say about making an offering out of this cup to any god? May I, or not?"

The man answered, "We only prepare, Socrates, just as much as we believe enough."

"I understand," he said, "yet I must pray to the gods to bless my journey from this to that other world. May this then, which is my prayer, be granted to me." Then holding the cup to his lips, quite readily and cheerfully, he drank off the poison.

Most of us had been able to control our sorrow. But now when we saw him drinking and saw too he had finished the draught, we could no longer control ourselves. In spite of myself my tears were flowing fast, so that I covered my face and wept over myself. I was not weeping for him, but at the thought of my own hardship in losing such a companion. Nor was I the first, for Crito, when he found himself unable to restrain his tears, got up and moved away, and I followed. And at that moment, Apollodorus, who had been weeping all the time, broke out into a loud cry which made weaklings of us all.

Socrates alone retained his calm. "What is this strange outcry?" he said. "I sent away the women mainly in order that they might not behave this way, for I have heard a man should die in peace. Be quiet then and have patience."

When we heard that, we were ashamed and stopped crying. He walked about until he said his legs began to weaken and then he lay on his back, according to the directions. The man who gave him the poison now and then looked at his feet and legs. After a while the man pressed his foot hard and asked him if he could feel and Socrates said, "No." Then he pressed his leg, and so upwards and upwards, and thus showed us that Socrates was cold and stiff. Socrates then felt himself and said, "When the poison reaches the heart, that will be the end."

He was beginning to grow cold about the groin when he uncovered his face, for he had covered himself up, and said, in what were his last words, "Crito, I owe a cock to Asclepius. Will you remember to pay the debt?"[1]

"The debt shall be paid," said Crito, "is there anything else?"

There was no answer to this question but in a minute or two a movement was heard and the attendants uncovered him. His eyes were set, and Crito closed his eyes and mouth.

Such was the end, Echecrates, of our friend, whom I may truly call the most wise and just and best of all men I have ever known.

Thinking about the Tour

1. Before we visit the final monument on our tour, we should look back on our journey. A good way to do that is to describe the main features of each dialogue and then discuss their similarities and differences.

I would divide the *Euthyphro* into ___ parts. In the first part Socrates is _____

_____

_____

_____. Euthyphro is _____

_____

_____

_____. The main features of the second part are _____

_____

_____

_____

_____. In the remaining sections

_____

_____

_____

_____

_____

_____

_____

_____ .

2. I would divide the *Apology* into ___ parts. In the first section
Socrates _____

_____

_____

_____

_____ . The second section begins when he
says, " _____

_____

_____

_____ ." In this part he makes the
following points: _____

_____

_____

_____ . The main features of the
remaining sections are: _____

_____

_____

_____

_____ .

3. You said the *Crito* was divided into three main parts.

For simplicity, I will agree. In part one _____

_____

_____

_____

_____. In part two _____

_____

_____

_____

_____. In part three _____

_____

_____

_____

_____. The major change in Socrates in
this dialogue is that he moves from _____

_____

_____ to _____

_____

_____

_____

_____. By the end, he is _____

_____

_____

_____

_____.

4. The main aspects of Socrates' personality we see in the death
scene of the *Phaedo* are: _____

_____

_____

_____

_____. Most importantly, when he says, "_____

_____

_____

_____

_____," we see he is _____

_____

_____

_____

_____. Examples of this in a previous dialogue might be _____

_____

_____

_____

_____

_____ .

Now, we need to think about the similarities and differences among the dialogues. A logical way to do this is to talk about what is unique in each dialogue (the differences), then what is common to most of the dialogues (the similarities).

The unique features of the *Euthyphro* are: _____

_____

_____

_____. What I learn about Socrates in the *Apology* that I really don't see in any of the other dialogues is:

_____

_____

_____

_____. New aspects of Socrates' character in the *Crito* are: _____

_____

_____

_____

_____. Additional new characteristics
at the end of the *Phaedo* are: _____

_____

_____

_____

—   _____

_____. Characteristics of Socrates that are
common to more than one of these dialogues are: _____

_____

_____

_____

_____

_____

_____ .

/5/ "ALLEGORY OF THE CAVE"

Preview

The "Allegory of the Cave" is a short section from the *Republic*, written during the middle of Plato's career. The *Republic* attempts to define the word *justice*, but in doing so presents Plato's view of the ideal State. In the following section, Plato describes his view of the structure of reality, the relationship between the philosopher and society, the stages of enlightenment, and the main features of the philosophical temperament.

Annotation Tasks

Main Theme. Underline the major symbols and Plato's explanation of them.

"Allegory of the Cave" (from the **Republic**)

SOCRATES: And now let me show you in a story to what degree we are enlightened or unenlightened. Can you see human beings living in a cave, which has a mouth open toward the light? Here they have been from their childhood and have their legs and necks chained so they cannot move. They can only see in front of them, being prevented by the chains from turning their heads around. Above and behind them a fire is blazing at a distance, and between the fire and the prisoners there is a raised walkway. You will see, if you look, a low wall built above the walkway like the screen which puppet players have in front of them, over which they show the puppets.

GLAUCON: I see.

SOC: And do you see men passing along the wall carrying all sorts of vessels and statues and figures of animals made of wood, stone, and various materials, which appear over the wall? Some of the men are talking, others silent.

GLAU: You show me a strange image, and they are strange prisoners.

SOC: Like ourselves, and they see only their own shadows, or the shadows of one another, which the fire throws on the opposite wall of the cave.

GLAU: True, how could they see anything but the shadows if they were never allowed to move their heads?

SOC: And of the objects which are being carried, in the same manner they would see only the shadows?

GLAU: Yes.

SOC: And if they were able to talk to each other, would they suppose they were naming what was actually before them?

GLAU: They would.

SOC: And suppose further the prison had an echo which came from the cave wall. Would they be sure to believe when one of the passers-by behind them spoke that the voice which they heard came from the passing shadow?

GLAU: Yes.

SOC: To them the truth would be literally nothing but the shadows of the images.

GLAU: That is certain.

SOC: And now look again and see what will naturally follow if the prisoners are released and their error is corrected. At first, when any of them is liberated and suddenly compelled to stand up and turn his neck around and walk and look toward the light, he will suffer sharp pains. The glare will hurt him and he will be unable to see the realities of which, in his former state, he has only seen the shadows. Then imagine someone says to him what he saw before was an illusion; but now, when he is approaching nearer to reality and his eye is turned toward more real existence, he has a clearer vision. What will be his reply? You may further imagine his instructor is pointing to the objects as they pass and requiring him to name them—will he not be confused? Will he not believe the shadows he formerly saw are truer than the objects which are now shown to him?

GLAU: Far truer.

SOC: And if he is compelled to look straight at the fire, will he not have pain in his eyes which will make him turn away and take refuge in the shadows which he can see, and which he will believe to be clearer than the things which are now being shown to him?

GLAU: True.

SOC: And suppose once more he is reluctantly dragged up the steep and rugged ascent, and held until he is forced into the presence of the sun, is he not likely to be pained and irritated? When he approaches the sunlight his eyes will be dazzled, and he will not be able to see anything at all of what are now called realities.

GLAU: Not all at once.

SOC: He will need to grow accustomed to the sight of the upper world. And first he will see the shadows best, next the reflections of men and other objects in the water, and then the objects themselves. Then he will gaze upon the light of the moon and the stars and the spangled heaven. He will see the sky and the stars by night better than the sun or the light of the sun by day?

GLAU: Certainly.

SOC: Last of all he will be able to see the sun and not mere reflections of it in the water, but he will see the sun in its own proper place, and not in another. And he will contemplate the sun as it is.

GLAU: Certainly.

SOC: He will then proceed to argue that this is what controls the seasons and the years, and is the guardian of all that is in the visible world, and in a certain way the cause of all things which he and his fellows were accustomed to behold?

GLAU: Clearly, he would first see the sun and then its nature.

SOC: And when he remembered his old dwelling and the wisdom of the cave and his fellow prisoners, do you suppose he would be happy about his change and pity the prisoners?

GLAU: Certainly, he would.

SOC: And if the prisoners were in the habit of conferring honors among themselves on those who were quickest to observe the passing shadows and to discuss which of them went before, and which followed after, and which were together, and who were therefore best able to draw conclusions as to the future, do you think he would care for such honors and glories or envy the possessors of them? Would he not say with Homer, "Better to be the slave of a slave," and to endure anything, rather than think as they do and live in their way?

GLAU: Yes, I think he would rather suffer anything than entertain those false notions and live in that miserable manner.

SOC: Imagine once more, such a one coming suddenly out of the sun and returning to his old situation. Would he not be certain to have his eyes full of darkness?

GLAU: Certainly.

SOC: And if there was a contest and he had to compete in measuring the shadows with the prisoners who had never moved out of the den, while his sight was still weak and before his eyes had become steady, would he not seem ridiculous? Men would

The major symbols Socrates has

established are: _____

_____

_____

_____

_____ .

In essence he seems to be

saying _____

_____

_____

_____

_____

_____ .

say of him that he left and returned without his eyes and that it was better not even to think of leaving. If anyone tried to free another and lead him up to the light, let them only catch the offender, and they would put him to death.

GLAU: No question.

SOC: This entire allegory you may add, dear Glaucon, to the previous argument. The cave is the world of sight, the light of the fire is the sun, and you will not misunderstand me if you interpret the journey upwards to be the ascent of the soul into the world of Forms, which according to my poor belief, at your desire, I have described—whether rightly or wrongly the god knows. But, whether true or false, my opinion is that in the higher world the Form of the Good appears last of all, and is seen only with an effort. When seen it is also inferred to be the universal author of all things beautiful and right, parent of light and the sun in this visible world, and the immediate source of reason and truth in the higher world. This is the power upon which he who would act rationally either in public or private life must have his eye fixed.

Now Socrates begins to interpret the Allegory. Underline each symbol he explains.

GLAU: I agree as far as I am able to understand you.

SOC: Moreover you must not wonder that those who achieve this wonderful vision are unwilling to descend to human affairs. Their souls are always hastening into the upper world where they desire to dwell. This desire of theirs is very natural, if our allegory can be trusted.

GLAU: Yes, very natural.

SOC: And is there anything surprising in one who passes from divine contemplations to the evil state of man, appearing in a ridiculous manner; if, while his eyes are blinking and before he has become accustomed to the surrounding darkness, he is compelled to fight in courts of law, or in other places, about the shadows of images of justice and is trying to answer the ideas of those who have never yet seen the Form of Justice?

GLAU: Anything but surprising.

SOC: Anyone who has common sense will remember there are two kinds and two causes of confused eyesight. These come either from coming out of the light or from going into the light, which is true of the mind's eye just as much as of the bodily eye. He who remembers this, when he sees anyone whose vision is confused and weak, will not be too ready to laugh. He will first ask whether the soul of that man has come out of the brighter light and is unable to see because unaccustomed to the dark or, having turned from darkness to the day, is dazzled by excess of light. And he will believe the one happy in his condition and he will pity the other. Or, if he wants to laugh at the one who comes from below into the light, there will be more reason in this than in laughing at one who returns from the light into the cave.

GLAU: That is a very just distinction.

The most interesting aspects of
this allegory are: _____

_____

_____

_____

_____

_____

_____ .

SOC: But then, if I am right, certain teachers must be wrong when they say they can put knowledge into the soul which was not there before, like sight into blind eyes.

GLAU: They undoubtedly say this.

SOC: Whereas, our argument shows the power and capacity of learning exists in the soul already. Just as the eye was unable to turn from darkness to light without the whole body, so too the mind can only by the movement of the whole soul be turned from the world of Change into that Unchanging reality, and learn by degrees to endure the sight of reality, and of the brightest and best of reality, or in other words, of the Good.

Thinking about the "Allegory of the Cave"

1. Imagine you have the task of explaining the "Allegory" to someone else. Start by making a stick figure drawing of the prisoners, the cave, the one who escapes, and the world outside. Label each symbol and also write in what it symbolizes.

"Allegory of the Cave" by _____ .

2. Here is a brief introduction to one of Plato's major contributions to philosophy. Two realms exist in the "Allegory," the cave and outside the cave. These symbolize the two realms of reality for Plato: the Changing and the Unchanging. The shadows in the cave symbolize all that changes in our world. Everything in the room you are sitting in will eventually change. Desk, walls, book, and paper will all change and eventually

disintegrate. Everything you know with your senses, in fact, will change and disintegrate. Mountains are no more stable, in the long run, than clouds. All these things, desks, chairs, books, mountains, and clouds are the Changing, the lower realm, the Cave of Shadows.

There is another aspect to reality as there is another part of the *Allegory of the Cave.* Plato maintained that a higher realm was Unchanging, and he symbolized this by the world outside the cave. The Changing realm is easier to understand than the higher Unchanging realm. It takes only a little reflection to see that everything you know with your senses changes—but is there anything Unchanging?

Would _____

_____ be examples of things that are Unchanging?

Think of it this way. Let us say you write the number 2 on this page, and then you erase it. What has happened?

You respond, "The number I wrote down changed. First it was there and then it was gone. But the number it was a symbol for, 2 itself, the idea of 2 in my mind, that was not erased. There are two 2s! One I see with my eyes, which is part of the Changing, and the one in my mind, which does not change, that must be Unchanging!"

Now, take this one step further. Plato believed that the 2 you see in your mind is eternal. If you and all humans died, the idea, or Form, of 2 would still exist. Where? In the higher, nonphysical realm of reality.

Now try to put this in your own words.

According to Plato, there are two levels to reality; one changes and the other doesn't. The level that changes is everything I know with my senses, the physical world, everything I can see, touch, taste, feel, and smell. Obvious examples of this Changing

realm are _____

_____ . The other level is Unchanging. This Unchanging level is something like the ideas I have in my mind, like the idea of 2 that is different from the physical symbol of 2 I might draw on a page. Plato calls these ideas Forms and they exist forever, even if there is no one to think about them.

Would some other Forms be _____

_____

_____ ?

Everything you know with your senses is a *copy* of a Form. Plato's great symbol for this was, of course, the shadows in the cave. They are imperfect copies of the objects behind the prisoners. Mountains, clouds, humans, apples, and chairs are all imperfect physical copies of the nonphysical, perfect Forms. Therefore, some other examples of perfect, unchanging, non-physical Forms would be the Form of Mountain, the Form of Cloud, the Form of Human, the Form of Apple. All things we know with our senses are imperfect "shadows" of these perfect essences. To be enlightened is to escape from the lower world of the cave or, more philosophically, the world of the senses, and ascend into a higher realm, the Unchanging realm of the perfect Forms.

This is not the place for an extended discussion of Plato's view of reality—that would involve a whole new tour. Let me just say this: Thales believed that reality was basically one kind of thing. The basic substance of reality, for him, was water. In the "Allegory," Plato holds that reality is basically two kinds of things. The lower level is Changing, and we know it with our senses. This he symbolizes by the world of the Cave. The higher level is Unchanging, and we know it with our mind, even though it is independent of our mind. This he symbolizes by the world outside the cave. One last example: good ice cream would be in the lower realm; the Good itself would be in the higher realm.

3. Look at the following list and decide which items Plato would classify as part of the lower world (the Cave of Shadows, the Changing, the world we know with our senses) and which as part of the higher world (outside the Cave, the Unchanging, the world we know with our minds). Use an "L" to indicate lower-world items, an "H" for higher-world items.

1. A wood desk
2. This book
3. The essence of holiness
4. The perfect circle
5. A beautiful sunset
6. Beauty itself
7. Sunset itself
8. The works of Einstein
9. The truth of the works of Einstein
10. A newspaper
11. Perfect justice
12. The Mona Lisa
13. The ideal woman
14. Socrates

15. These words

16. A courageous action

17. The essence of courage

18. Our Constitution

19. The gods

20. The words in the dictionary that define *wisdom*

21. What the words in the dictionary refer to when they define *wisdom*

I hope you find some of these obvious and some debatable.

Platonist Test

What do you and Plato agree on? Plato believed some of the following statements were true. Decide what your position is and then read the evaluation on pages 121–123 to see how much of a Platonist you are.

1. T or F: The soul is immortal.

2. T or F: Rule by the wise, not democracy, is the best form of government.

3. T or F: Might makes right.

4. T or F: The physical universe is the only reality.

5. T or F: The mind can know truths independently of information from the senses.

6. T or F: Our reason exists to effectively serve our desires.

7. T or F: The majority of people are foolish.

8. T or F: In a just society, all people would share equally.

9. T or F: We should have faith that God exists.

10. T or F: We never, truly, learn anything new. All wisdom is recollected from a time before our birth.

11. T or F: If the realm of Forms didn't exist, the physical universe wouldn't exist.

12. T or F: All knowledge in our minds came through our senses.

13. T or F: All of reality is constantly changing.

14. T or F: There are two levels to reality: the lower, physical level is a copy of the higher, nonphysical level.

15. T or F: The ideal society would be ruled by a philosopher-king.

16. T or F: The ideal society would be ruled by a philosopher-queen.

17. T or F: Perfect beauty exists.

18. T or F: Perfect courage exists.

19. T or F: Perfect justice exists.

20. T or F: The highest principle in reality is the essence of Goodness.

21. T or F: Nothing for certain can be known about anything that changes.

22. T or F: The body is the prison of the soul.

23. T or F: Virtuous people are rare.

24. T or F: If triangles didn't exist, then the Form of triangle wouldn't exist.

25. T or F: A true philosopher is regarded as a fool by the majority of people.

/6/ BENEATH THE SURFACE OF THE DIALOGUES

Philosophy, according to Aristotle, begins in wonder. I encourage you now to wonder about what more can be discovered in Plato's dialogues. If you remember nothing else about Plato from this book, please remember this: There is always more to be discovered.

In Plato's works I find that three questions help me get beneath the surface of a dialogue. First I ask: What connects the arguments? This is a question about the philosophical content of the dialogue. Second, I ask: How does the dramatic situation in the dialogue change? This is a question about the theatrical content of the dialogue. Third, I ask, logically enough: What is the relationship between the philosophical and the theatrical in this dialogue? My experience has been that wondering about the answers to these questions often reveals a hidden structure beneath the surface of Plato's works.

Let us use the *Euthyphro* as an example. If this dialogue is only about holiness, then, in some sense, it is a failure. No definition is reached. Let us see what more can be discovered.

First, think about the connections between the arguments—in this case, the definitions of the holy.

The first six definitions might be stated as follows:

1. Holiness is bringing a justifiable murder charge against one's father.
2. Holiness is what the gods love.
3. Holiness is what all the gods love.

4. Holiness is a kind of moral rightness.

5. Holiness is a trading skill between the gods and men.

6. Holiness is what is dear to the gods.

Answering the following questions, may help you begin to find a hidden structure among the definitions.

1. Of the six, which definition is the least general; that is, the least like a definition? (1, 2, 3, 4, 5, 6). Why?

_____

_____

_____

_____

_____ .

2. At which definition does Euthyphro start to rely on traditional knowledge of the gods? (1, 2, 3, 4, 5, 6). Why?

_____

_____

_____

_____

_____ .

3. At which definition does Euthyphro have to abandon traditional knowledge of the gods? (1, 2, 3, 4, 5, 6). Why?

_____

_____

_____

_____

_____ .

4. At which definition does Euthyphro return to his knowledge of the gods? (1, 2, 3, 4, 5, 6). Why?

_____

_____

_____

_____

_____

_____ .

5. What is established by the *Euthyphro?* (Choose one of the following.)
   a. There is a realm of values, like holiness, dependent on the gods.
   b. There is a realm of values, like holiness, independent of the gods.
   c. There are no gods.
   d. There are no values.

6. What is the "trajectory" of the *Euthyphro?* What connects one definition to another, and what hidden order do these definitions make? (Choose one of the following.)
   a. The definitions in the *Euthyphro* move from the general to the specific and back to the general again.
   b. The definitions in the *Euthyphro* move from the specific to the general and back to the specific again.
   c. The definitions in the *Euthyphro* move from the specific, up to the traditional realm of the gods, and then toward a still higher realm of values independent of the gods before falling back on a more traditional approach to the gods.
   d. The definitions in the *Euthyphro* move from the general, back to the specific, then toward the traditional realm of the gods, and then toward a still higher realm of values dependent on the gods before finally defining holiness conclusively.

From my point of view, the correct answers are: 1, 2, 4, 6, b, c.

Now, think about the dramatic content of the *Euthyphro,* and then perhaps we can tie the philosophical to the dramatic.

How does the dramatic relationship between Socrates and Euthyphro change during the course of the dialogue?

Early in the dialogue Euthyphro is _____

_____

_____ and Socrates is _____

_____

_____

_____ . I would describe their

relationship as _____

_____

_____

_____

_____. Toward the middle of the dialogue Euthyphro is _____

_____

_____ and Socrates is _____

_____

_____

_____. At this point, their relationship

is _____

_____

_____

_____. By the end of the dialogue,

Euthyphro is _____

_____

_____

_____. Socrates is _____

_____

_____

_____

_____. At the end I see the two of them

as _____

_____

_____

_____.

Now, you have thought a few moments about how the definitions change and about how the two men and their relationship

change. Although you may not think so, you are beginning to see beneath the surface of the *Euthyphro*. You are beginning to see that Plato's philosophy is dynamic. Philosophy, for him, is an activity and not simply a set of beliefs. Some philosophers seem to carve their views into granite; Plato floats his upon a deep and shifting river. The river is the fluctuating, dramatic tension between Socrates and his partners.

Can you see Socrates gradually taking more and more control of the relationship and the course of the definitions in the *Euthyphro*? One idea that will unite the dramatic and the philosophical is to view the dialogue as a philosophical therapy. Socrates is trying to cure Euthyphro of a complex illness. Euthyphro's attitude toward himself, Socrates, his father, the gods, and the members of the Assembly are all symptoms of his illness. His first definition is a clear outbreak of this illness. You might be able to see successive definitions and the major shifts in their relationship as stages in a cure attempted by Socrates. Euthyphro isn't cured, of course, but the dialogue gives many hints as to what the cure involves. You might think of the "Allegory of the Cave" as a more extended analysis of the illness and the paradoxical cure. In fact, a great paper would compare and contrast Euthyphro's journey and that of the escapee in the "Allegory of the Cave." In Chapter 7 I suggest methods for constructing this paper as well as several less ambitious efforts. Believe it or not, you have already done most of the hard work.

/7/ WRITING ABOUT THE DIALOGUES

Most philosophy teachers want their students to do one or more of the following four kinds of writing:

1. Paraphrase philosophical arguments
2. Criticize philosophical arguments
3. Compare philosophical arguments
4. Apply a philosophical argument to a contemporary situation

Paraphrasing

Paraphrasing simply involves putting an argument into your own words. You have already paraphrased several of Socrates' arguments.

Let us say your instructor asks you to paraphrase the "Allegory of the Cave." First, make a list of the main points you want to establish. Then think about the list. Are the points in the right order? Are there any points missing? Then write a few simple introductory sentences. Most philosophy teachers want you to get right to the point; they know Socrates was a great philosopher and that he lived long ago in Athens. Avoid retelling history. Here is the beginning of a short essay, paraphrasing the "Allegory of the Cave."

"The Allegory of the Cave" is divided into two main parts. In the first part, Plato tells a symbolic story, using the following as symbols: _____

_____

_____

_____

_____. In the second part, he
explains each symbol.

The rest of your paper would then fall into two obvious sections. Tell the story in your own words, and mention each of the
symbols in the same order as your first sentence. Then explain
the significance of each symbol in the second half of your paper.

Criticizing a Philosophical Argument

To criticize an argument you must be able to paraphrase it.
Make two lists. In the first list, write the points you need to make
to summarize the argument as you just did. In the second list,
write the points from the first list that you think are the weakest. Think about your lists. What have you left out?

Now go back and think of quotations from the argument and
where you want to insert them on your list. Think of examples
that will illustrate your points and place these on your list. Think
about the list again. What have you left out? Copy the list over
if it is a mess. Juggling ideas in a list is far easier than juggling
them in a paper.

Think harder about criticizing the argument. Your teacher
wants evidence and, usually, the more the better. Fortunately,
Plato provides great examples of how to criticize arguments. Look
back at your notes on the *Crito* and the *Euthyphro*. Socrates states
his points and then usually illustrates them with one or more
examples. Look at the examples you have on your second list.
Improve and clarify them.

Your teacher might ask you to criticize any two of Socrates'
reasons for remaining in jail. Here is how you might begin:

Socrates' two weakest reasons for staying in jail are: _____

_____

_____

_____. The main problem with the first

reason is _____ ⁄ _____

_____

_____

_____

_____ . His second reason is weak because

_____

_____

_____

_____ . (Then expand Socrates' reasons and
your criticisms in the body of your paper, using your two lists.)

Comparing Philosophical Arguments

Teachers love this assignment. It is one of the most compli-
cated to write, but if you use a list your task will be easier. Here
is a take-home essay: "Compare Euthyphro's journey with that
of the prisoner who escapes from the Cave. Use material from
other dialogues where pertinent."

Remember you can make and revise a list far easier than you
can write and revise a paper. This question suggests two lists: a
list of similarities between Euthyphro and the prisoner and a list
of differences. However, a good job would also summarize the
"Allegory of the Cave" and the main features of the *Euthyphro*.
Proceed as follows:

1. List the points you need to summarize the "Allegory of the
   Cave."
2. Do the same for the Euthyphro.
3. List the similarities.
4. List the differences.
5. Think of examples from the *Apology* and the *Crito* that will tell
   the reader more about Socrates or someone like Euthyphro.
   Insert these examples in list 3 or 4.

Consider the lists. Cross out weak points; add stronger points,
find quotations from the dialogues and insert them in the correct
places on your lists; recopy the whole thing. Consider it again.
Add and delete quotes; think of original examples; add and delete

points. Take a break, and then write a few simple introductory sentences, such as:

There are _____ main similarities and _____ main differences between Euthyphro's journey and the prisoner's journey in the "Allegory of the Cave." (Add one sentence for each similarity and each difference. Begin the body of the paper with a summary of the *Euthyphro*, followed by a summary of the "Allegory of the Cave." Then allow about one paragraph for discussion of each similarity and difference. Take another break, revise everything you wrote, and proofread.

Applying Philosophy to Contemporary Situations

- Would Socrates be a draft resister?
- How would someone who interprets the Bible literally define holiness?
- What new arguments could you offer Socrates to get him to escape?
- Compare the life of Socrates with Gandhi's or Martin Luther King's.

You should have an idea about how to proceed on any of these subjects. Yes, make a list. In general the first items on your list should be points about Socrates and examples from the dialogues. Then list the points you want to make about the specific question. Revise your list; add original examples; add, delete, and rearrange points.

One more good suggestion that applies to all philosophical writing is to talk to someone before you begin. Most teachers welcome the chance to clarify successful and unsuccessful approaches to an assignment. Explaining your approach to someone not in your class often helps you see the task more clearly. Instructors often encourage students to talk to one another about assignments. Talking is the only thing easier than making lists.

APPENDIX A:
A VISUAL
INTRODUCTION
TO PHILOSOPHY

Philosophy can be defined as the study of the nature of wisdom. But this definition presents a problem. What is wisdom? Wisdom is certainly some kind of knowledge. But what kind?

Most people would probably agree that wisdom is knowledge about large, rather than small, issues. The time of day is a small issue; the nature of time is a large issue. Where you're going tonight is a small issue; where you're going with your life is a large issue. Knowing the truth about your neighbor is a small issue; knowing the nature of truth is a large issue.

A good way to see the difference between small, non-wisdom issues and larger, wisdom issues is to state each as questions.

- How do I know that Ignacio is my friend?
- **How do I know anything?**
- Does God listen to my prayers?
- **Does God exist?**
- Will I be happy as a plumber?
- **What is happiness?**

In philosophy we deal with the boldfaced, wisdom-producing questions . . . the large issues. Note that each plain-text question assumes one already has at least a partial answer to the boldfaced question below it. Asking "How do I know that Ignacio is my friend?" assumes you can answer the larger question **"How do I know anything?"** If you wonder if God hears your prayers, you have assumed that the answer to the second question **"Does God exist?"** is yes. Pondering the happiness of a plumber's life implies that you know what happiness is.

In philosophy we burrow through the small questions of daily life to get at the large, dark questions underneath. A philosopher is a truth mole. Take the case of happiness.

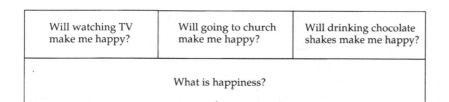

Will watching TV make me happy?	Will going to church make me happy?	Will drinking chocolate shakes make me happy?
What is happiness?		

During daily life, a philosopher might worry about the top-level questions, the small issues. When she is engaged in philosophy, however, she tries to answer the large question that her smaller questions rest upon. To put this more philosophically, when we adopt a philosophical attitude we search for supporting evidence for our assumptions about reality, knowledge, and human life.

Now, give me an example of a small question.

_____

_____ ?

What is a related larger question?

_____

_____ ?

In order to answer the first question I would have to ____

_____

_____ .

But, in order to answer the second question I would have to

_____

_____ .

Because there are many kinds of wisdom questions, philosophy has many branches. Three of the major branches of philosophical inquiry are diagrammed here.

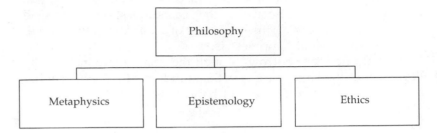

Metaphysics

In metaphysics we ask questions about the nature of reality. Is God real? Does the soul exist? Does the physical world exist or is it just an illusion? If you had answers to these questions, then you would have wisdom about the nature of reality or, as philosophers sometimes put it, the nature of Being. Note the contrast between the following small questions and the larger metaphysical questions.

- Are my keys in the drawer? (Do my keys exist in the drawer?)
- **Does anything but the physical universe exist?**
- What kind of person am I?
- **What is human nature?**
- What is the answer to this math problem?
- **If human minds didn't exist, would numbers still exist?**

The plain-text questions are the questions of daily life, small issues that come and go. The boldfaced questions are metaphysical and enduring. They ask about the nature of the universe, human beings, and what does and does not exist. To engage in metaphysics is to dig down through small questions into large questions about the nature of reality.

When Socrates says that the unexamined life is not worth living, he means that life among the small questions has no value. He spent his life happily tunneling through the philosophical underground.

One way to tell if you are attracted to philosophy is to ask yourself if any of the boldfaced questions listed here interest you.

My answer is ———— because ————————————

——————————————————————————————————

——————————————————————————————————.

Give me your own example of a nonmetaphysical question you might ask yourself during a normal day and the deeper, metaphysical question it is based on.

_____

_____

_____

_____ .

I wouldn't want you to think that philosophers ask large questions and don't answer them. Their attempts to answer metaphysical questions are determined by which of the two branches of metaphysics they accept.

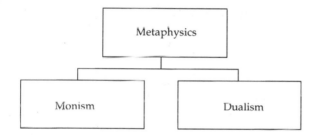

Monism is the view that all of reality is one kind of thing. For example, Thales, the first philosopher, and Karl Marx, the father of communism, were both monists. Thales held that the essential element of reality was water. Trees, mountains, clouds, and humans all had water as their basic element. Thales never said how this could be. How water was at the root of all that existed was a boldfaced question he never answered. Marx held that God, heaven, hell, and the human soul were illusions generated by the upper class to make the lower class forget the pain of life in an unjust society. Religion, according to Marx, is the pain-numbing opiate of the masses. From his point of view, there was nothing to reality except matter. Humans are soulless flesh and bone. There is no higher world. There is no father in the sky. Nothing exists but the hard, challenging world around us.

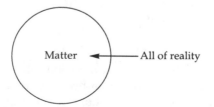

Dualism is the view that all of reality consists of two kinds of things. Both Plato and St. Augustine were dualists. Plato held that all of reality was divided between the realm of Forms and the physical universe. The world we see around us is a shadow, a flickering shadow, of the higher realm of Forms. Today's apple is tomorrow's garbage, but the essence of Apple is Unchanging, sweetly eternal. Augustine held that all of reality was divided between the realm of God and the human realm. We live in the dark human city, a metropolis of sin, confusion, and error. We aspire to the Eternal City where the divine sun never sets on God's goodness.

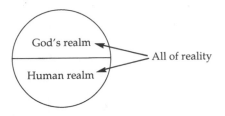

Now, you know a very small amount about metaphysics and its branches. Tell me what you have learned.

Well, _____

_____

_____

_____ .

Epistemology

In epistemology we ask wisdom questions about knowledge. These questions are not about the information we hold in our minds but about how that information got there and whether any of it is reliable.

- Who is playing in the Super Bowl?
- **How do humans acquire knowledge?**
- How do I know that Gunter loves me?
- **How can I be certain of anything?**
- How can I learn to play tennis?
- **How does anyone learn anything?**

Whereas in metaphysics we ask questions about what is real, in epistemology we ask questions about how we come to have knowledge about the real. If God is real, how did that information come to me? If God isn't real, how did that information come to me? Another way to put this is to say that in epistemology we ask questions about how the knower knows the known.

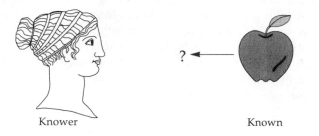

Knower   Known

In general, there are three answers to the question about how the knower knows the known. *Empiricism* holds that the knower knows the known through the senses. *Rationalism* holds that the knower knows the known independently of the senses. *Skepticism* holds that the knower can't know the known with or without the senses.

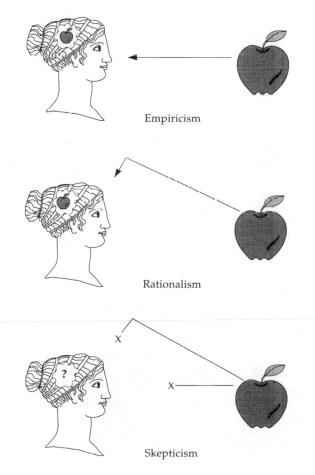

Empiricism

Rationalism

Skepticism

Let's think briefly about each kind of epistemology.

If I am an empiricist, then I hold that all knowledge comes to me through my senses. Everything that is in my mind came in through one of five avenues: sight, hearing, touch, smell, or taste. A scientist is an empiricist. She believes that telescopes and microscopes are tools for learning about reality.

Aristotle, known as the Father of Science, was the first great empiricist. He used his senses to gather and organize information about the physical world and founded the sciences of biology, botany, and geology, among others.

Give me some examples of information you believe you learned empirically.

_____

_____ .

A rationalist holds that the senses are not reliable. If your friends fooled you once, you might never fully trust them again. Your senses have fooled you many times. In fact, every night your senses deceitfully convince you that you are wandering in a bizarre land. Rationalists take dreams and other examples of sense errors as good reasons not to trust the reports of the senses. Rationalism argues that you have five liars glued to your body. Ignore what they tell you.

But if we don't gain knowledge through our senses, then how do we acquire it? Two rationalistic answers are:

- We are born with knowledge already inside our minds.
- God puts knowledge directly into our minds.

Plato held the first view. The knowledge that we are born with is the knowledge of the Forms. We are born with this knowledge because our souls, prior to birth, existed in the realm of Forms. Augustine held the second view. Whenever we know something for certain, it is because God is illuminating our mind. God is the sun that allows the eye of our mind to see. Studying the Pythagorean theorem, our senses see that the square made from the long side of a right triangle is equal to the area of the squares made from the other two sides. God enlightens our minds to see that this is true of all right triangles—even those in Zanzibar.

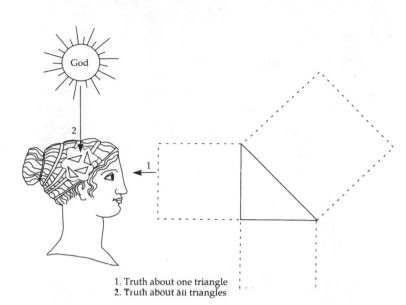

1. Truth about one triangle
2. Truth about all triangles

Do you have any knowledge that you believe you were born with or that God put directly into your mind sometime during your life?

I would say _____

_____

_____.

A skeptic holds that all that I've said about epistemology is wrong. There is no way the mind can gain knowledge. All we know are half-truths and unfounded assumptions. The senses deceive us and the mind certainly does not have access to God. We are born empty-headed and fill our skulls with falsehoods we believe are true. The mind is an error bank.

You've now heard, very briefly, about three branches of epistemology: empiricism, rationalism and skepticism.

Which makes the most sense and why?

_____

_____

_____.

Ethics

In ethics we ask questions about the nature of right and wrong human actions. How should we live our lives? What is good for us to do? What is bad for us to do? What is an ideal human being? What is true happiness? Note the contrasting questions.

- Should I tell Mary about Gunter?
- **Is it always right to tell the truth?**

- What movie should I go to?
- **What is the highest pleasure?**

- How can I be happy?
- **Is happiness possible?**

All the choices you make in life are founded on hidden ethical questions. If you decide to pursue a teaching career, it is obvious that you think that is the right choice for you. One hidden ethical question is, Are some goals better to pursue than others? Another hidden ethical question is, Should all people do whatever they wish? A third hidden ethical question is, Do individuals have any obligation to help other individuals?

Give me your top-of-the-head answer to any one of these questions.

I think _____

_____ because _____

_____ .

You just engaged in an ethical inquiry.

Two of the many branches of ethics are *hedonism* and *asceticism*. Hedonism is the view that physical pleasure is right. Asceticism is the view that physical pleasure is wrong.

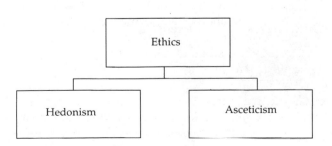

Eat, drink, and be exceedingly merry. That is a short formula for hedonism. Pursue the joys of the senses. Do whatever gives you physical delight. If I gave you the assignment to be "Hedonist for a Week," what would you do?

_____

_____

_____ !!!!

An ascetic holds that physical pleasure is wrong. It pollutes the mind, corrupts the soul, and leads to pain, not pleasure. According to both Plato and Augustine, bodily pleasures are dangerous things. Plato held that you can never satisfy your bodily appetites. Trying to do so is wrong because you let desire rule reason. In other words, you let the most foolish part of your nature rule the wisest. That is a formula for philosophical suicide. Augustine held that the body is the domain of sinful cravings. Give in to the body's desires and you are led away from God. Indulging in physical pleasure makes it impossible to indulge in the highest pleasure, spiritual communion with the Divine.

Well, are you a hedonist or an ascetic? And why?

I would describe myself as _____ because _____

_____ .

In general I think a person should seek _____

because _____

and avoid _____ because _____

_____ .

Conclusion

Philosophy is the study of the nature of wisdom. In metaphysics we try to gain wisdom about the real and the illusory; in epistemology we try to gain wisdom about how and what we know; in ethics we try to gain wisdom about what we should and shouldn't do. Now, how do all three of these fit together?

Plato provides a good example. In *Platonic metaphysics*, reality is divided into two parts, the higher realm, which is the province of the Forms, and the lower realm, which is the province of the physical universe. In *Platonic epistemology*, our senses provide us with no reliable knowledge about the lower realm because the physical universe is constantly changing. We are, however, born with genuine knowledge because our souls existed prior to birth in the realm of the Forms. *Platonic ethics*, therefore, states that what we should do with our lives is reject the attractions of the physical world, let our reason rule our appetites, and pursue wisdom by purifying our souls with the study of philosophy.

Helping you do that is what this book is about.

Fill in the rectangles of the following diagram with these words: philosophy, metaphysics, ethics, epistemology, monism, dualism, rationalism, empiricism, hedonism, asceticism. Attach the following philosophers to the correct boxes in the diagram: Plato (3 boxes), Augustine (3 boxes), Aristotle (1 box), Thales (1 box), Karl Marx (1 box).

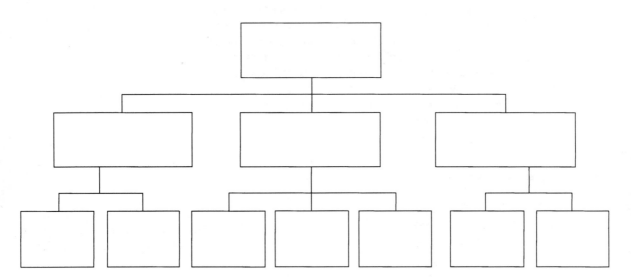

APPENDIX B:
PHILOSOPHY AND SELF-KNOWLEDGE: KEEPING A PHILOSOPHICAL DIARY

Perhaps you would like some suggestions about how to continue the tour on your own. One of the central characteristics that Euthyphro, Meletus, and Crito share is an inability to criticize their own views. Each lives in his own Cave. They cannot wonder—I suggest you practice wondering.

Wondering is not dreaming, and it is never satisfied with its first observation. Wonder is fueled by questions that criticize conclusions. In the *Euthyphro* Socrates is a wonder machine. Wonder drives beyond the first, second, and third answer; goes beyond the shadows; and hunts relentlessly for the bright world of Unchanging Truth.

Even my brightest students are poor wonderers. For example, after they have described Euthyphro, I might ask "Now, what is wrong with what you just said?" Their faces are marvelously blank. The essence of wonder is wondering what is wrong with what you just said. Truth never comes off the top of your head, or if it does, you have a fine opportunity to wonder why.

If I ask you to think about God or the Holy or Socrates, you would probably say what you believed was true and stop rather than wonder. You don't need practice in thinking; you need practice in thinking about what is wrong with your thinking.

To really wonder, you need a subject about which you have a great deal of information. The only thing you have a lifetime's worth of experience about is your life. Here are a series of questions you can fruitfully wonder about in a philosophical diary. (Some of these questions touch on issues or concepts you just read about or may hear about in your philosophy class.)

- *Who am I?* (This is the central question—the remaining questions will help fuel your wondering.)
- What has changed in my personality since childhood?
- What has not changed in my personality since childhood?
- What is good about me?
- What do I mean by the good?
- What is bad about me?
- What do I mean by the bad?
- Where does the good and bad in me come from?
- What is it that I hold in common with my father? With my mother? With all members of my family? With many other humans? With God?
- What are the differences between myself and my father? And my mother? And all members of my family? And all humans? And all life? And God?
- What has remained the same in my relationship with my father, mother, sister, brother?
- What has changed in each of these relationships?
- What evidence do I have about what has changed and what has remained the same in these important relationships?
- What were the turning points in my life? How did they influence me?
- In what ways have I changed for the better? For the worse?
- Why do I believe what I believe about any of the above? How do I know it is true?
- What can I be certain of about myself?
- About what, or whom, have I been really wrong in my life? What led me wrong? What can I learn from that?
- What lessons has life taught me?
- What lies was I told?
- What illusions have I held?
- What generalizations can I make about myself, my father, mother, family members, or friends? What is my best evidence for these generalizations? What do I believe about

any of these people that is not true? How did I arrive at such an error?

- How would I define *love, responsibility, foolishness, wisdom?* What examples from my own life would support this definition?

- What people have had the greatest influence on me? What did they give me that I lacked or needed? Was their influence good or bad? Again, what do I mean by "good" and "bad"? How have I learned what these words mean?

- What is wrong with my responses to all these questions?

All these questions will help you wonder about the first question, Who am I? Keep asking yourself what is wrong with what you just said. And when you draw a blank, become suspicious, not content.

Eventually you will come to ideas that seem solid, that feel like bedrock. This is what you are after—answers purified by deep wonder. Live with them awhile, and come back and wonder about them later.

For many of you, this is the end of your first text in philosophy. Let me know its strengths and weaknesses. I wish you ceaseless wonder on the rest of your journey.

NOTES

Chapter 1

1. The Lyceum was a popular area of Athens where Aristotle would later establish his school. The king archon was a judge who presided over trials involving religious issues.

2. Zeus was the ruler of the Greek gods; Cronos was Zeus' father, who was killed by Zeus; and Uranus was Zeus' grandfather and first ruler of the Universe, killed by Cronos. The "nameless manner" of his death involved castration.

3. The Panathenaea is an Athenian religious festival held once every four years.

4. Hephaestus is a Greek god and the deformed son of Hera, a Greek goddess.

5. Daedalus was a legendary master craftsman.

6. Tantalus, despite his great wealth, was sentenced to dwell in Hades by Zeus for his crimes. In Hades, he stood knee-deep in water that receded when he tried to drink, beneath branches of fruit too high for him to reach.

7. Stasinus is a poet about whom nothing is known except this quotation.

Chapter 2

1. The comic poet is Aristophanes, mentioned in the first chapter of our tour.

2. Gorgias, a skeptic, Prodicus, a sophist, and Hippias, a general know-it-all, are contemporaries of Socrates.

3. Evenus the Parian is a poet and specialist in rhetoric whose fee is about $1000.

4. The god of Delphi speaks through a female oracle who passes into a trance after sitting above a fissure in the earth from which gases escape. The messages are frequently paradoxical.

5. "By the dog" is a favorite comic oath of Socrates.

6. Herculean labors refer to the legendary hero, Hercules, who was sentenced to twelve great labors for killing his wife and children.

7. Anaxagoras was an eminent philosopher who was also tried for impiety.

8. The son of Thetis is Achilles, hero of Homer's *Iliad*.

9. "As Homer says" refers to a quotation from his *Odyssey*, the story of Odysseus' return from the Trojan War.

10. The Prytaneum was a building maintained by Athens to provide lodging and food for important visitors and particularly deserving citizens.

11. Minos, Rhadamanthus, Aeacus are the mortal sons of Zeus; they lived so justly that they were given the honor of being judges in Hades.

12. Orpheus and Masaeus were legendary poets. Hesiod, author of *Works and Days*, was a close contemporary of, and nearly equal in reputation to, Homer.

13. Palamedes and Ajax are heroes of the Trojan War.

14. Sisyphus is the king of Corinth who was sentenced for his disrespect by Zeus to eternally push a boulder up a hill only to have it roll down again.

Chapter 3

1. Phthia was the home of Achilles. The dream probably meant to Socrates that dying meant returning home.

Chapter 4

1. Asclepius is the god of health. Crito's offering would then mean Socrates regarded death as the cure for the illness of living.

Platonist Test Evaluation

I've underlined what I believe Plato's answers would be.

1. <u>T</u> or F: The soul is immortal.
2. <u>T</u> or F: Rule by the wise, not democracy, is the best form of government. (This is Plato's position in the *Republic*.)

3. T or <u>F</u>: Might makes right. (Thrasymachus holds this view in the *Republic,* and Socrates refutes it.

4. T or <u>F</u>: The physical universe is the only reality. (The "Allegory of the Cave" argues that the physical world is only the lower, and less real, part of reality.)

5. <u>T</u> or F: The mind can know truths independently of any information from the senses. (Many of Plato's dialogues, but especially the *Meno,* hold this.)

6. T or <u>F</u>: Our reason exists to effectively serve our desires. (The philosopher David Hume held this view, but Plato certainly didn't.)

7. <u>T</u> or F: The majority of people are foolish. (This could be supported from the "Allegory of the Cave.")

8. T or <u>F</u>: In a just society, all people would share equally. (Plato takes the view in the *Republic* that the lower classes should have the wealth. The upper classes would be content with the gold and silver in their souls.)

9. T or <u>F</u>: We should have faith that God exists. (Plato says nothing about faith and very little about anything we would understand as "God.")

10. <u>T</u> or F: We never, truly, learn anything new. All wisdom is recollected from a time before our birth. (Plato elaborates this view in many dialogues.)

11. <u>T</u> or F: If the realm of Forms didn't exist, the physical universe wouldn't exist.

12. T or <u>F</u>: All knowledge in our minds came through our senses. (According to Plato, sense knowledge is only knowledge of "shadows.")

13. T or <u>F</u>: All of reality is constantly changing. (Heraclitus held this but not Plato.)

14. <u>T</u> or F: There are two levels to reality: The lower physical level is a copy of the higher nonphysical level. (Plato is a dualist.)

15. <u>T</u> or F: The ideal society would be ruled by a philosopher-king. (According to the *Republic*)

16. <u>T</u> or F: The ideal society would be ruled by a philosopher-queen. (Plato, taking an advanced view for a Greek, says in the *Republic* that women could rule his ideal state.)

17. <u>T</u> or F: Perfect beauty exists.

18. <u>T</u> or F: Perfect courage exists.

19. <u>T</u> or F: Perfect justice exists.

20. <u>T</u> or F: The highest principle in reality is the essence of Goodness. ("Allegory of the Cave")

21. <u>T</u> or F: Nothing for certain can be known about anything that changes. (This is one of Plato's fundamental principles.)

22. <u>T</u> or F: The body is the prison of the soul. (Plato's *Phaedo* contains eloquent arguments for this view.)

23. <u>T</u> or F: Virtuous people are rare. (Few people want to be led out of the Cave or are capable of the difficult ascent.)

24. T or <u>F</u>: If triangles didn't exist, then the Form of triangle wouldn't exist. (This is the exact opposite of the theory of Forms.)

25. <u>T</u> or F: A true philosopher is regarded as a fool by the majority of people. (The "Allegory of the Cave" supports this view.)

For each question that you and Plato agree on, give yourself 1 point. Score as follows: 23–25: Plato would be happy to have you teach in his Academy. 20–22: Plato would hold that you are on the right track but probably need work in abstract reasoning. Take a refresher course in geometry. 15–20: You're in danger of corrupting your soul with foolishness. 10–14: Welcome to the Cave. 5–9: Welcome to the Cave basement. 1–4: Form a Euthyphro fan club. 0: In your next life, you'll be reborn as a slug.

RECOMMENDED READINGS

By Plato

Plato. *Meno.* R. S. Bluck, ed. and trans. Cambridge University Press, 1961. This is probably less difficult than *Euthyphro* and should pose no problem for you. Socrates begins by considering whether Virtue can be taught, but digresses toward the middle to demonstrate that Wisdom is never learned but only recollected from a time before birth.

Plato. *Symposium.* Kenneth Dover, ed. and trans. Cambridge University Press, 1980. Socrates and his friends drink all night and have a contest about who can give the best speech on Love. Simple enough at first reading and endlessly complex thereafter.

Plato. *Republic.* Francis Cornford, ed. and trans. Oxford University Press, 1968. This translation has superb notes that will guide you, with patience, through Plato's most philosophically comprehensive work. If you have the feeling after the present tour that Plato never really spells out his beliefs, read the *Republic*. All the big answers are there.

Plato. *Phaedo.* Any modern translation. Most of this will cause you no difficulty. About one-fourth requires close reading and rereading and is a fine place to practice skills you learned on the tour. In his last hours, Socrates spells out the relationship between the body and soul and is challenged by two fellows far brighter than either Crito or Euthyphro.

About the Period

Jones, W. T. *The Classical Mind.* Harcourt, Brace, 1952. A superb overview of the Greeks that is also the first volume of a brilliantly readable history of philosophy. For further reading, look into Jones's suggestions at the end of the text.

Renault, Mary. *The Last of the Wine.* Pantheon, 1956. Few novels on any subject match her account of Athens in the days of Socrates.

Richter, Gisela. *A Handbook of Greek Art.* Phaidon Press, 1959. Sculpture and architecture are a convenient way to revisit the age of Socrates and Plato. Richter's book contains abundant illustrations of one of the most beautiful worlds humans ever created.

Now that you've finished this tour I would be very happy to hear what you think of it. Write me:

> Christopher Biffle
> Crafton Hills College
> Yucaipa, California 92399

or send me a message on CompuServe, (73602,2060).